MAINTAINING

MOTIVATION

Designing a Balanced Successful Life

By Matthew D. Mohr

Dacotah Paper Co.
Copyright © 2002

All rights reserved. No part of this publication may be reproduced or transmitted in any form or by and means, electronic or mechanical, including photocopying, recording, or by any information storage and retrieval system, without permission in writing from Dacotah Paper Co. or the Author.

Library of Congress Control Number: 2001098928
ISBN 0-9709251-1-5
MG
Printed in the United States of America

Additional copies may be ordered from:
    Dacotah Paper Co.
    P.O. Box 2727
    Fargo, ND 58102
    (800) 323-7683

FORWARD

A heartfelt thank you to the many employees of Dacotah Paper Company who all continue to support me in my quest for Entrepreneurial excellence, while at the same time giving me the opportunity to pursue my many passions in life including this book. My success in life would be incomplete without all of you.

A special thank you to Marcia Hagen, my Executive Assistant, who in a very short time has accepted the many quirks of my personality. Who took my handwritten, miss-spelled pages with enthusiasm and coordinated the publishing of this work. Without her, this book and my last would have probably languished.

DEDICATION

To my son Benjamin;   Best friends, confidant, brilliant winner, one of my biggest fans. May you find your way through life with great joy and many accomplishments, you are destined for greatness.

To my son Caleb;   Best friends, kamikaze kid, enthusiastic spirit, one of my biggest fans. May your love for life remain with you forever. Always discovering joy, you are certain to inspire many in this world.

To my daughter Berea;   Constantly curious, a young shining star, still finding your way. You are meant to brighten the days of those who pass your way.

INTRODUCTION

Throughout this book various aspects of life are explored to help guide you towards a more fulfilling life based on your individual desires.

The life principles explored and the aspects of daily living were chosen to provide a broad base of options for the reader to explore in his or her own life.

The object of this book is to help you define what is most important in your life so you can consciously determine what actions will lead you to a state of daily enjoyment. Upon completing your first reading, you should feel an internal desire to accomplish more of what is truly important in your life to you.

Table of Contents

Chapter 1:   MOTIVATION 7

Chapter 2:   LIFE'S BALANCE 11

Chapter 3:   THE FREIGHT TRAIN 13

Chapter 4:   PHYSICAL 16

Chapter 5:   MENTAL 22

Chapter 6:   GOALS 26

Chapter 7:   FINANCIAL 28

Chapter 8:   CAREER 40

Chapter 9:   COMMUNITY 44

Chapter 10: FAITH/HOPE 46

Chapter 11: RELIGION 49

Chapter 12: CHARACTER 53

Chapter 13: THANKFULNESS 56

Chapter 14: HELP 59

Chapter 15: TEMPTATIONS 63

Chapter 16: ETHICS AND INTEGRITY 65

Chapter 17: HONESTY 72

Table of Contents (continued)

Chapter 18: TEACHING 76

Chapter 19: PERSONAL RELATIONSHIPS .. 81

Chapter 20: WINNING 89

Chapter 21: STRESS 92

Chapter 22: ATTITUDE 97

Chapter 23: GOALS; SEGMENT 2 99

Chapter 24: BALANCE CHALLENGE 106

Chapter 25: SELF-DISCIPLINE 111

Chapter 26: DIRECTION 114

Chapter 27: CHOICE 115

Chapter 28: MORE THOUGHTS 116

Chapter 29: DAY BY DAY 118

Chapter 30: ACTION IDEA'S 121

Chapter 1

MOTIVATION

'Some people sit under the banana tree waiting for the fruit to fall, while others climb the tree to get the fruit when they want it.'

Some people seem to contain boundless energy and the capacity to get things done. Other people drift along from day to day seldom doing more than enough to get by in life.

Why does one person with no more ability than the next person achieve so much more in life? The answer comes from the ability to generate self-discipline to create enthusiasm within for accomplishment. Motivation occurs by the conscious decision to take action. Nothing is accomplished until someone takes action. Action only occurs through self-determination. Interest in life is brought about by personal desire.

By taking action, you create desire. By reading this book you are starting to take action, and you can begin to balance your life to find personal fulfillment during the time you spend on this earth.

To achieve anything you want in your life, you must begin to take action to move you closer to your desired outcome.

To graduate from college, get a good job and start a career, you must decide which college is best for you, and then you must do your best to start classes at a college of your choice.

Motivation

Few people would choose the challenging difficulty of attending a school of higher learning if they didn't envision a better life resulting from their education. The desire to take action comes from the belief positive results will flow to you from your better education. The willingness to maintain the discipline to attend class day after day is created by this desire. The achievement of a good education is an excellent example of personal motivation.

Motivation comes from within, it occurs when you believe a positive outcome will result for you from your actions.

Permanent motivation is the internal drive to grow and move forward. Sometimes a book, a speech, or an event can help create a temporary spark or create a continually burning flame to help motivate a person.

Basically, there are two types of motivation. One is reward motivation, the other is fear motivation. Both have their place and either can create a strong desire within you. Either can lead to great accomplishments. Your preferred motivation style is largely dependent on your experience in life and what you deeply desire as an outcome for your life.

Most of today's motivation experts focus solely on reward motivation. It's show up for work, do a good job, and you'll get a pay raise. The thousands of people pitching retirement plans use

Motivation

reward motivation almost solely. They rarely talk of the possibilities of loss, only talk of the financial riches their subscribers will receive by investing with them. If only it were that easy, we would all be millionaires.

Reward motivation focus is effective, but the rewards can only grow so large. You begin by paying your son 10 cents to clean his room, as he gets older you raise the reward to fifty cents, then a dollar, and so on. How long or how high can the reward go? You must find a level of reasonableness, so that the rewards given closely match the achievements. Low achievements should translate to low rewards.

Fear motivation, on the other hand, has its place as well. It's the factor which says, work hard or you're going to get fired. I know a mother who tends to use fear motivation or punishment almost exclusively with her children. The smallest infraction to her rules can end up with some punishment for her children. Fortunately she seems to be non-violent. Her punishments are no television, stay alone in your room, no candy for a week, and the like. Think of how challenging it must be for her children to always be threatened with some loss. She wonders why her children don't respond positively to her. Unfortunately for her and her children this punishment orientation has lead to multiple arguments within her family. She has missed the point of how to find a balance between punishment and reward.

Motivation

Most successful people have an internal motivation or desire for success. Seeing your deepest desires realized are the best way to create positive self-worth.

Every situation demands a judgment between rewards and punishment. Maybe any punishment is just too negative for you. To be an effective motivator or to keep yourself continually striving for personal excellence you need to strike a balance between reward and fear motivation. Find your balance and you will discover real success.

You can argue punishment doesn't work. After all, our prisons today are overcrowded with inmates serving time for breaking the rules of our society. The fear of punishment by imprisonment didn't stop the crime. Obviously the rewards of a good, free life didn't stop the crime either.

If you are not, have been previously, or have not been in jail, you probably are not in jail presently because you have established for yourself the punishment of jail time is too high, and the rewards of freedom are too good to give up. It is both the reward of freedom and the punishment of imprisonment that keep you out of jail.

Complete motivation in life requires both positive and negative aspects. Utilizing only one type usually will not work. You need to employ both.

Chapter 2

LIFE'S BALANCE

' Tomorrow awaits – take your place!'

In one way or another, everyone works for the right balance for living an enjoyable life as they define for themselves. Each person chooses to pursue their balance based on their individual desires, wants and needs. No two people view life the same. Each person is motivated in different ways.

In most cases, a drug addict is a highly motivated individual. We can see this motivation through their constant desire to achieve another fix or acquire more of the item of their addiction. Nothing can stand in the way of an addict. Many addicts loose sight of reality and morality to feed their addiction. Addiction creates bad motivation resulting in bad actions.

An intelligently motivated individual will assess life to discover their personal desires and through this process create a balanced life for themselves.

A positively balanced life only occurs by purpose. You determine what is important in your life. By consciously seeking a balance, we are able to guide ourselves to a more fulfilling existence. Your thoughts, actions, and desires will propel you to that which you value most. Make your desires good, positive, productive. This will

Life's Balance

usually create a life where your actions match those good positive productive desires.

Perhaps at this early point in this book you are saying to yourself...my life is great right now, I have a good balance. If this is the case, you may be right, but I suggest you look around quickly because you are probably standing right in the path of a speeding freight train!

From this point forward we will explore new areas for your life's experiences. We will explore new ways to create self-motivation and action. I urge you to read on!

Chapter 3

THE FREIGHT TRAIN

'Lilies look a lot nicer when you're standing above them, than when you are six feet below them.'

The year 1998 began as most years. I spent time reviewing my accomplishments of the previous year, and began writing my plans and goals for the future. For some reason I reviewed my last 20 years of goal planning sheets. I had achieved nearly every major goal I had set over the past 20 years. My life was grand and in good balance. I had a great family, and my health was seemingly perfect. My career was stimulating, fun, and rewarding. I was teaching Sunday school and felt I was spiritually strong. Financially I was secure. Mentally I continued to read and grow beyond my formal education. Needless to say, I did not expect to face the challenges I would endure the following months.

The freight train arrived on March 20, 1998, when I suffered a massive stroke and subsequently spent seven weeks in Merit Care hospital in Fargo, North Dakota.

A stroke affects each person in different ways. Essentially, a stroke is caused either by a blood clot which blocks blood flow to the brain, or the bursting of a blood vessel in the brain, which eliminates proper blood flow to the brain. In each case, the victim faces some level of brain damage. My particular stroke was caused by a

The Freight Train

blood clot, which resulted in the loss of a large portion of the right side of my brain, considered to be a major stroke. Shortly after the time of my hospital admission, it became evident to my family that I might not be able to walk or work again. Life was hanging by a thread, modern medical miracles were employed to save me.

My life's balance was shattered in a few moments. Once I regained consciousness, the many aspects of my life had to be reevaluated. I had long believed in living a life by my own design. Now that design had crumbled. It was time to pick up the pieces to reestablish myself. Fortunately I was confident life would go on and life could become better for me, believing the freight train wreck would soon be cleaned up, with the train sent back on its way for the next unsuspecting soul.

To find a new balance, it was time to start a focus on the physical attributes of my life. So my life now involved a new challenge, it was up to me and my family to face reality or be overcome by it.

Recognizing I needed a lot of additional exercise or physical therapy, We also recognized there was no quick fix for me. Exercise had to become a new focus in my life. Every day for the first few months following my stroke, Cynthia escorted me to a hospital gymnasium. Neither one of us really wanted to go to that gym day after day. Imagine having to struggle to move a few pound barbell. Hating to have any dependence on anyone for

The Freight Train

help, the gym time together took its toll on both of us. As soon as I regained some independence, Cynthia stopped helping me at the gym and I was put on my own. It was not much better being alone, but it had to be done if my physical health would ever return. The only option for success involved work and prayer. As time progresses, the work and prayers remain as a part of our daily lives.

Chapter 4

PHYSICAL

'The day was a happy one, when I finally could hold my baby girl in my arms.'

We are all endowed with different physical attributes. As humans we have the choice to exercise or not, eat right or maintain poor nutrition. Most plants grow as strong as possible given the environment in which they are placed. The human body will grow as strong as it can, given its genetics and the nutrients it receives. Unfortunately many of us don't put into our bodies the right fuel. We frequently forgo the right exercise. We opt out for soda pop, chips, chocolate bars, and television.

A well-balanced life requires a commitment to good food along with proper exercise. Your food intake is critical to how you feel. Sugar coated breakfast? Expect a definite good feeling for a few minutes. Expect a real lethargic feeling in an hour or two.

If you smoke a pack of cigarettes a day you hurt yourself and those around you. Every puff takes you closer to your grave. Alcohol has seen a lot of press. Perhaps one reasonably sized drink a day can do you some good. A pint of whiskey every morning is not good and will hurt your life.

There are hundreds of books available on nutrition. Unfortunately, most are full of technical information when all we really want to know is

Physical

what to eat. You should explore nutrition to determine what is best for your lifestyle. Pick a good food intake plan (diet), stick to it for a reasonable time to assess how the food plan affects you. Maybe two pieces of fruit a day will do you good. Two cans of soda pop will probably do you harm.

In today's environment too much emphasis is given to excessive exercising. Everyone needs a different level of exercise. There is no one-exercise program that fits all of us. You need to test for yourself how your body feels after differing levels of exercise. Maybe a light one-hour walk once or twice a week is best for your body. Maybe two or three hard workouts at a gym is what will suit you best. The only way to determine what you need is through testing. Start out with an exercise program which includes a variety of light exercises. Be sure to include exercises you like and those you don't like. If you can, employ the help of an exercise physiologist so you learn the right ways. A good yearly physical is a must. A cardio-vascular check every three years is also a must. One thing is certain about exercise, and that certainty is; you must do some exercise every week. Walk, run, bicycle ride, do something to get your blood moving or you will face the negative long-term health effects of no exercise.

My physical health always seemed excellent. I felt little need to push my body. After my stroke, I needed to reassess my position about personal exercise. We searched for the cause of my stroke; blood disorder, heart trouble, cholesterol,

Physical

what caused this catastrophe? Finally we concluded I had been born with a heart defect, which had gone undetected. The defect seemed too small to be of immediate concern. During what I thought would be a routing examination at the Mayo Clinic in Rochester, Minnesota, I was told I needed open-heart surgery as fast as possible. The surgery was performed, and as a consequence, it was time to reassess exercise again.

For months life included a routine at the hospital gymnasium as we tried to assist my body in its rebuilding. Now it was going to be time to start all over! Luckily, for this challenge, we saw the freight train headlight in time to get out of the way, we corrected the problem by taking action before the next catastrophe.

Physical health is not always controllable. You may be involved with a serious accident, you can get tuberculosis without even knowing how you contracted it! Fortunately we have a fantastic medical system and many wonderful treatments available today. You are responsible for your health and you can take action to feel stronger, better, more physically fit.

During my 7-week post-stroke rehabilitation stay at Merit Care Hospital in Fargo, ND, a man was in physical rehabilitation with bandaged hands and feet. He had a very negative attitude. Thinking he had been badly burned I tried to overlook his bad attitude and somewhat befriended him. Months later, we met again in outpatient hand therapy. He

Physical

informed me he had contracted some unusual, uncorrectable staff infection which spread to his hands and feet. His hands looked horrible. His hands were swollen, sore, and seemed to be pretty much useless. A few months later, we met again as he arrived at outpatient therapy. The area manager asked how he had done at Rochester. He smilingly replied two "B-K".

Having no idea what a B-K meant, after inquiring I learned he had both feet amputated below the knees! He was starting a process of breaking each bone of each hand in an attempt to restore some use of his hands. From a bad attitude with an infection to prosthetic feet and broken hands, he moved from swearing to smiling. We cannot always control the physical health we have, but even in the most extreme cases, we can take action, even if painful to improve ourselves.

How good would your attitude be with no feet and seemingly useless hands? Today, this man is one of my mental hero's. Using his image generates thankful motivation.

Available for your use are many excellent books on food, diet and exercise. Once again, you are unique, no one else can tell you how to reach your optimum physical state. Seek a physical level you enjoy. To find the right physical balance, acquire a few good books (and read them) as you start to grow your knowledge about diet and exercise. With the right motivation, no physical mountain is insurmountable.

Physical

In our community lives Judy Siegle. She is a very bright woman. She works at MeritCare Hospital and has had to overcome a major physical battle in her life.

Judy was a shining basketball player, who was named a Minnesota All-State player in high school. After high school, she planned for a great basketball career at Concordia College in Moorhead, Minnesota. The summer after high school, prior to starting college, she was involved in a terrible automobile accident. The accident left her a quadriplegic, initially paralyzed from the shoulders down.

Judy is not the kind of person to wait for life to find her, she embraces life each day. She faced horrible odds. How could she overcome such a tragedy for a spirited athlete?

Judy went to work on herself. She fought for a way to find a complete life. She fought so hard that she has become a world-class wheelchair Olympic athlete. In 1999, Judy won two gold medals in wheelchair racing at the Pan-Am games in Mexico City, Mexico, earning herself worldwide recognition for her accomplishment.

Today, Judy still makes physical exercise part of her life. Despite being classified as a quadriplegic, she has started to regain some muscle strength. Against every medical opinion she is moving herself forward.

Physical

Does every day take a lot of work for Judy? You bet it does. She constantly works herself physically, and must maintain an optimistic mental attitude to have a positive life in her wheelchair. Judy continues to use her positive motivation with her mind to overcome her physical limitations.

Maybe you are not ever going to have such a tragic accident like Judy. Could you face the odds? Could you put forth the effort necessary to beat the odds? You can, if you have the right mental attitude.

Today, if you do enjoy good physical health, you should assess your life, take action to maintain your long-term health, and expand your personal knowledge of nutrition and exercise.

Chapter 5

MENTAL

'One is far better off not being able to remember, than not being able to forget'

Each of our mental abilities are a wondrous mystery. We were the one animal given great minds; minds strong enough to create our own environment. The power of choice to alter our environment is one of the great benefits we have over other animals. We are the only living being which can choose to grow our abilities.

When the human observed the bird flying in the air he began dreaming of the day he could fly. After centuries of dreaming man made the airplane. Today we hop on an airplane to soar from one end of the earth to the other. Someday we will soar from our end of the Galaxy to the other, just as we dream about it today. We wanted to swim to the deepest depths of the Oceans, so we invented the air tank and submarine.

Currently less than 5% of the American population owns a library card. Yet it seems we all want a credit card!

You have the ability to grow, learn, and the chance to pursue a better life.

Does anyone know everything about anything? If you think you do, you don't. When feeling sick, most everyone wants to see the very best doctor available. A doctor who stops reading about medicine the day of graduation from Medical School will fail. A doctor is expected to grow far beyond the formal education of Medical School. We all should have the same expectations of continuous education of ourselves for life.

Our world shows respect to education by providing greater monetary rewards to those who use their education in the best manner to serve our society. Granted a few professions do take long, hard years of education, but receive small monetary rewards, but most professions requiring the greatest educations provide the highest rewards.

After graduating from college, during his first year of marriage, a good friend of mine took the time to read an entire dictionary. Not many of us have the personal commitment to grow our vocabulary by reading a dictionary. This man has used his mind to expand his world view, his language and vocabulary skills are extraordinary which helps him succeed in life. During this first year of marriage, his bride was perplexed at this "weird" man she was with. Many, many people accused Thomas Edison of being crazy to keep working on the light bulb after he had spent years in his laboratory. Few of us would dismiss Edison's work today. Yes, grow your mind, become weird, perhaps you'll discover the Edison within you.

To create enthusiasm and the desire to pursue excellence in your profession, you must grow. The

Mental

best opportunity you have for growth is through expanding your mind.

During the sixth grade our class was told our IQ's based on some standard national testing. One of my friends at the time received the lowest score in the class, and was supposedly below the national average. Other children criticized him, laughed at his stupidity and chastised him. He was always friendly and considerate to me and the other kids. His family eventually moved from our school district, but I never forgot this very considerate friend. After 30 years of not speaking to him I acquired his phone number and called him. Today, he is a very successful business manager. He holds responsibility for over 50 adults. One of the people I work with was previously employed at the same firm as my old, low IQ friend. My fellow employee informed me in an unbiased way this man is very respected, considered very bright, and always did a top rated job. Had he let his seemly low IQ stop him, 50 families would be out of work today!

Far too often we let other people categorize us. The world is full of examples of people going beyond their society imposed limits. You can develop your mental abilities and grow far beyond the limits someone else tried to impose upon you! Expand your mind and expand your understanding of your world.

Much of our understanding of life comes from how we interpret our world. The greater a person's vocabulary, the deeper understanding the person

Mental

can have of their life's events. How we interpret our world is based largely on our vocabulary. If you only know two words for how you feel, these being happy and sad. You live a bi-polar existence. Add to your vocabulary, words such as depressed, excited, thrilled, fearful, enthralled, hopeful, bored, fulfilled, and you will have a much greater life.

One of the greatest elements of our mind is our ability to experience life through the learning of the experiences of others. How fascinating it is to be able to learn from Bill Gates [Microsoft Corp] by reading his books. Would you not be thrilled to learn from Abraham Lincoln himself! You can learn from Lincoln because hundreds of books exist about his life. The Gettysburg Address is available to you word for word. You can read the Gettysburg Address given by Lincoln and hear it in your mind just the same as those who attended the speech decades ago.

Reading, growing your mind, gives you a sense of accomplishment, expands your horizons, and can provide great enjoyment in life.

Use you mind, grow your mind, and grow your life's experiences through learning. While it is important to devote the right amount of time to learning, you must use what you have learned. A teacher who spends all day reading, but neglects to share her knowledge with her students has gained nothing and is not better off than the person who never entered a classroom.

Chapter 6

GOALS

'If you don't know where you are going, any road will take you there.'

Goals are critical for accomplishment. Everyone must have goals. The best goals are written down and communicated to others.

When my oldest son was 9 years old he entered a longest drive contest at our country club during the Fourth of July celebration. The club pro had a youth 'Ping' driver available so Benjamin tried it. He hit the furthest he ever had that day. He had the longest drive of the youth boys until he was overtaken by two boys thirteen and twelve years old. At the end of the contest, the club pro suggested Benjamin announce to the crowd "that Ping driver works pretty good Dad". By then Benjamin was hooked on the Ping driver. He wanted a new driver, and his Dad really wanted his son as a lifetime golfing buddy.

Purchasing the new driver for Benjamin as a gift would have been very easy. However, a great opportunity to teach him about goals was at hand.

After careful consideration together we decided, if Benjamin would ask for and accomplish a household job everyday for three solid weeks, he would earn himself that new golf club. For three weeks, Benjamin did every job he was assigned without complaint, and as a result he was presented with his new Ping driver.

Goals

This example contains the essence of the goal setting process. First the goal was meaningful to Benjamin (a new golf club). We established what needed to be done to achieve the goal. The goal had to be earned and we set a specific time for accomplishment. Finally he is enjoying the fruits of his labor by owning and using his new club.

My rewards came from having a lot of household jobs cleaned up. Even bigger rewards will follow from both of us enjoying more meaningful golf together. Benjamin has now learned the value of goal setting, which will provide him lifelong accomplishments along with a much more productive life. I have a much desired golf buddy.

Goals are much easier to accomplish if you write them down. Goals take on many shapes and should be of substance to you. All goals are important, but in our society financial goals are very important to your long-term happiness.

Chapter 7

FINANCIAL

'Money doesn't give happiness, but money can provide access to a lot of opportunities for happy times.'

Money is the resource which everyone in our society needs to have in order to insure their basic necessities are met. Financial resources also provide access to opportunities to enhance your life.

Is the woman who earns $100,000 per month better than the woman who earns $100.00 per month? The answer depends upon your personal values. We can easily argue the woman who earns the greater amount is providing greater value to our society. Monetary rewards do follow the value society perceives you provide. If the woman who earns $100.00 is earning all she can, she is a success. If the woman who earns $100,000.00 could earn $500,000.00 she is a failure.

Perhaps, you have chosen a profession in life which doesn't provide you the monetary rewards you seek or feel you deserve. You can change! You can take action to change your profession. Changing professions, going back to school, looking for a new job involves significant risk. But to find the right long-term balance in your life, you need to take action! Don't think some outside force will suddenly discover you are worth much

Financial

more. You choose your profession and employer. You must take responsibility for your financial future by taking action yourself.

Teachers today often complain they are underpaid for the contribution they provide. Perhaps this is true; Teaching provides great internal satisfaction (rewards). Teaching allows a certain desirable lifestyle (personal time, work environment, etc). Teaching also results in a particular set of financial rewards. Financial rewards in a chosen profession cannot be the only point of focus. Every career has its benefits. Admiration for teaching is detailed in a separate chapter in this book.

Many teachers have moved to other professions, some are highly successful, others have failed.

A certain high school teacher/high school athletic coach of my acquaintance in Chicago felt he needed to achieve greater financial rewards. He quit his high school teaching job, tossed out his hard earned education, then found a job in sales. He immediately doubled his take home pay. His take home pay today is roughly five times what his Chicago teachers salary would be. The trade off for him has been a fourteen-hour workday, and not seeing a high school sporting event for five years. Today, he has found the right profession for his life, allowing him the financial rewards he desires. Rather than complaining about his job, he took action and is now highly motivated to produce results in his life.

Financial

Regardless of what you choose to do for your employment, you must decide what value money plays in your life and seek to earn the rewards necessary for you to feel financially balanced.

Perhaps this Chicago high school teacher gave up too much of his personal life. By changing his work place, he now has the feeling of financial balance he wanted in his life.

Achieving financial balance takes hard work, risk and a commitment to do whatever it takes to receive the rewards you desire in life.

At one time in my life a very energetic woman came to me frustrated with her lack of financial success. We reviewed her financial situation. She had chosen a low-paying profession, which she loved. She did not want to change careers. Her internal rewards in her job were just too high to consider loosing. After careful analysis, we discovered she always paid the minimum amount due on her credit cards, resulting in exorbitant interest charges. We put together a six-month credit card pay-off plan. She found a second job in retail services to enhance her income. After six months her credit cards were all paid off. In three years she bought herself a new vehicle. In five years she bought herself a new sports car.

Was it worth it to sacrifice her nights for a retail job? She took the effort and found more financial success than she believed possible in her life.

Financial

This experience in my life was greatly rewarding as I observed this person achieving her financial goals. She had to commit to a plan. Despite her low-paying profession she took action (secured a second job), to enhance her financial position. Along with her financial rewards she kept her very satisfying profession in tact. She found financial balance in her life. She enjoys huge rewards in her life knowing she took action and succeeded!

Credit cards can be a wonderful financial tool, but they can also create financial disaster. Unfortunately, before we worked out a plan for her together, the woman I mentioned above did not understand the true cost of credit card interest. Today, credit cards offer purchase rebates. Credit cards can allow you to plan your cash outflows in concert with your cash inflows, which may result in much smoother cash flow for your life. Credit cards are great, but you must understand how to use them to your advantage.

Beyond credit cards, you may have bank debt, but you also have many assets at your disposal, which you use to enhance your life.

In our society, money is a necessary ingredient to a fulfilling lifestyle. Those who think they live well without money are foolish. Living a life without money in our society is possible, but you merely get by. Does the thought of plain bread for breakfast, lunch by begging, dinner at the Salvation Army sound like a great life? You

Financial

certainly can find a pair of shoes, an old blanket, a crust of bread, live under a bridge, and get by.

The gal who thinks that once she has a million dollars she will be happy is confused. It's a happy gal who takes the right steps to achieve the million-dollar goal.

One of my very best friends is financially secure, has the financial resources necessary to live a life of leisure. During a conversation he explained, "my original plan was to buy a Mercedes convertible when I became a millionaire, then it was two million." The realization of knowing he could buy the car of his dreams was enough to fulfill his desires. Up to this day, he has not bought his Mercedes or any convertible car for that matter. Knowing he can is enough. He doesn't have to show it to prove it. If he does buy a convertible, it will be solely for his personal enjoyment, not a statement of his wealth.

This same, very wealthy man works everyday, strives to grow his business and produces greater benefits for our society. He also explained to me one day "upon reaching the point financially of being able to live off my interest income, the realization came that my career was too much fun to give up to clipping bond coupons." It should not be the pure financial aspect you seek, but the rewards should come from the benefits to society you create. Create more benefit to society and society will financially reward you.

Financial

Hundreds of books exist on financial planning. I'm sure your local library has a few financial planning books which you can borrow to get you on track to a better financial life. Check a couple of these books out.

We are lucky to live during a time of relative financial stability. The thought of the average person employing a financial planner would have been considered ridiculous only one generation ago. Yet today, we have the faith our financial system will remain intact.

A particular experience of mine, which often reminds me of how fortunate we are to live in America, occurred one sunny afternoon in Seattle, Washington. After a meeting ended early, with a little extra time before sunset, it was time for me to see the Seattle wharf. On the way to the fish market a man was begging for money on a street corner. Most people ignored him, including me. Exactly one block past him on the ground was a dime, nickel, and two pennies. Three hundred feet from the beggars chosen station lay in waiting more money than he probably collected every hour. I picked up the seventeen cents. The beggar was still on his corner when I returned from the wharf. The seventeen cents stayed in my pocket! Had he taken the effort to move just three hundred feet, he would have found this money. Do you hear him crying; "the rich get richer, us poor just get poorer!"

Your financial dreams will be different than anyone else's financial dreams and desires. You

Financial

need to determine for your life what will keep you satisfied financially and what financial resources are necessary to provide you the life you desire.

Complete financial security occurs when you achieve true financial independence. Financial independence is reached when you do not need to depend upon anyone else (a job, a relative, the government) to provide you with money to acquire your daily necessities.

To build financial independence a person needs to have a strong group of financial assets. You are probably asking, where do you start? The best way to build assets is to start saving every month. As you save, allocate your savings equally among the asset pillars which follow on the next page. Any amount each month is acceptable. Perhaps you can not put aside enough to buy 100 shares of stock in Microsoft your first savings month, find out what you can save and invest your stock portion in just a few shares of stock. Don't expect to have all you need without a number of years of effort.

You should never go after the big win. Don't think you can outsmart the market by buying a security for pennies on the dollar. If you are offered a "golden opportunity" to invest in a business, be skeptical. Ask why no one else has become rich on this deal. No smart business owner is going to give you a portion of his gold mine.

Financial

No matter what the economic conditions, if you have a balanced portfolio of assets divided roughly amongst the following asset pillars, you will experience financial strength. When your earnings from your non-employment pillars is enough to provide you with significant enough disposable income to pay your living expenses, you will be financially independent.

FINANCIAL PILLARS

- Your Employment Income
- Marketable Common Stocks
- Fixed income saving instruments (CD's, corporate bonds, government savings bonds, bank savings account)
- Real Estate (Including your personal residence – if owned or mortgaged)
- Collectables (Must be easily sold if that becomes necessary)
- Retirement Accounts

You will notice financial pillars do not include your clothes, furniture, jewelry, car, boat, stereo or the like. True financial assets are those things you own which have a ready market and can be turned into cash in short notice.

No one can tell you what you should own. Perhaps owning CD's is a better fit for your risk

Financial

tolerance. If you can't take the wild swings of the public financial markets, there are many options which can lead you to financial independence.

Start by saving what you can each month. Maybe its' only possible for you to save $50.00 per month. After twelve months you will have $600.00. Put $200.00 into a bank savings account, pay down your home mortgage by $200.00, and find a stock broker to help you with a stock fund for the remaining $200.00. As your ability to grow your savings, the dollars invested will multiply quickly. Before you know it you will be saving $500.00 per month, then $5,000.00 You will discover with the right discipline, financial savings multiply, then your assets start to grow exponentially. Eventually you will be financially independent.

You need to establish solid financial goals, determine what material possessions are most important for you to acquire. Put your material possessions into a list by priority.

Most people strive to first acquire a personal residence, and then go on to other financial assets such as stocks and bonds. Your home is very important to consider in your overall financial plan.

If you are serious about putting your financial affairs in order, you can begin by taking some rather simple steps. First achieve a copy of your current credit report. A credit report will cost you $15.00 to $25.00 and must be made available to

Financial

you from your local credit bureau. Any discrepancies you find in your credit report should be corrected. Generally a letter with reasonable supporting documentation will be sufficient to cause the credit bureau to make the appropriate changes.

After acquiring your credit report, make up a personal net worth statement. List your assets and your liabilities. Assets are items of monetary value you possess. Liabilities are debts you owe to others. On the next page is a simple net worth statement you can use to start.

ASSETS:
Cash, Checking Account	$ _____
Common stocks you own	$ _____
Indebtedness to you	$ _____
Savings Bonds/CD's	$ _____
Cash Value of Life Insurance	$ _____
Personal Residence	$ _____
Retirement Accounts	$ _____
(IRA, 401K, Profit Sharing)	$ _____
Collectable Items	$ _____
Furniture	$ _____
Jewelry	$ _____
Other items of Value	$ _____
	$ _____

TOTAL ASSETS $ _____

LIABILITIES:
Credit Card balance due	$ _____
Automobile Loan	$ _____
Home Mortgage	$ _____
School Loans Payable	$ _____
Other Debts	$ _____
Other Miscellaneous amount owed	$ _____
	$ _____

Total Liabilities $ _____

NET WORTH
Total Assets - Total Liabilities $ _____

Financial

By determining your personal net worth you have calculated a place to start setting your financial goals. Assess what financial position you aspire to in your life.

Critical to achieving financial goals is your employment. Review your career aspirations to see if your career can provide you the desired financial rewards you seek.

If you are married, talk seriously about your financial goals together. Work together and start a plan of success.

Chapter 8

CAREER

'Any job well done is better than a job left undone.'

Most people expect to spend 40 hours per week on the job. Pursuing a solid career is a good activity for your life. For some reason our society has started to consider work as bad. The engines of commerce allow our society to create new levels of enjoyment for every one.

Your work or your job is not bad! Only you can make your job become bad in your mind.

One does not need to look back very far in history to find many great advancements to mankind created through a persons career. Our cities are brightly lit at night, and our air is much cleaner due to the efforts of Thomas Edison and many others of his era.

A job is a great thing to desire and obtain. A real career is fantastic. To truly find a balance in your life you must find a career which stimulates your interest and stimulates you to be productive. Do you really want to spend 1/3 of every hour of every one of your days unhappy at work?

Evaluate what activities make you feel good about yourself. What type of environment do you enjoy? Does being outside make you feel your best? Do you love the thought of commanding a big mahogany desk?

Career

Changing your career choice is a stressful, scary decision. Many people in the Fargo area recognize the real estate business name Goldmark. Jim Wieland, a very good friend of mine, is a principle of Goldmark.

Jim was determined to be a college professor. He loved the academic environment. After finishing graduate school and spending time doing both research and teaching at the college level, Jim recognized his lifetime career choice would not be completely fulfilling. He also had a keen interest in real estate, so he made the choice to change careers. To the dismay of his relatives, Jim left a comfortable lifetime career in education to be a commissioned real estate agent.

Leave a comfortable $40,000 to $60,000 a year job for the risk of a commission only real estate job? His father thought Jim had gone nuts.

Today, Jim and his partners enjoy enormous success with Goldmark. My guess is that Jim's yearly income is far superior to that of the best of College professors.

Additionally, Jim's contribution to our society far exceeds what his contribution would have been as a college professor. Goldmark's real estate development activity has provided countless jobs; they provide shelter (for rental) to hundreds of families in our community. There is no doubt about the good to our community Jim has made in his real estate career far exceed the contributions he would have made in a career as a teacher.

Career

Perhaps the thought of being a driver of an eighteen-wheeler semi-truck gives you a sense of success. If you can imagine the enjoyment of the open road, seeing the country, having the freedom to roam, then maybe this career is for you.

One of our former truck driving employees came to me one year requesting a job in sales. He viewed this as a promotion from his truck-driving job. I suggested this was a potential opportunity, but first he needed to go to school to take a couple of classes on sales, then after he had some education, he needed to demonstrate his desire to sell by getting a part-time job at a retail store. By following these simple two suggestions, he probably would get his sales job. This wouldn't work, he explained, because he really could do a job in sales, he thought he deserved the promotion. You already know he didn't go to school, didn't get a part-time job, and didn't get promoted. A few years later he asked me to write a letter of recommendation for him to go to school to become a minister. I did write the letter, he was accepted in school, but never attended! He obviously wasn't happy as a truck driver, but he wasn't willing to take the action necessary to change.

Do you like the idea of standing in front of a congregation leading prayer? Maybe a career as a minister is for you. You decide, you take action, no one can change but you.

Career

This book is far too short of the ability to be your career counselor. Other books and people are available to assist you in your career choice.

Your job is your choice. Find one you like and find one that fits your personality and make it into a true career.

Most truly successful people enjoy their careers. Successful people don't view their jobs with distain, but consider their work an enjoyable part of every day.

Without a successful career, it is hard to keep your faith during life's many challenges. The right career for you is out there, so find it! If you are an unhappy truck driver, do something to change your life! If you can't take the risk of changing jobs, try volunteering in your community.

Chapter 9

COMMUNITY

'Build a bridge between yourself and your fellow man and you will discover a new harmony exists in your world.'

Regardless of your chosen station in life, you can and should give to your community. Your donations to charity make the world better for you and everyone.

Giving of yourself requires sacrifices. The easiest thing to give is money. Time, on the other hand, is much harder to give to community organizations in need. In a small town like Fargo, ND, opportunities always exist to give of yourself. Regardless of where you live, you can provide help to those in need. For every successful project, thousands of hours go into its creation and completion. What is holding you back from giving some of yourself for the benefit of others? Discover for yourself some of the great joy of growing by donating. Without a doubt, you will build new relationships within yourself. You will also create new personal friendships through your community activities.

Bruce Furness, the Mayor of Fargo, I consider a personal friend. We met through a common commitment to Fargo's growth through the local Chamber of Commerce. We both helped mold the direction of the Chamber by championing an early strategic plan for that organization. Had we both not volunteered our time, we would not have

Community

become friends.

Bruce does a fantastic job as our Mayor. During the terrible flooding of the late 1990's, Bruce was able to keep a clear head, make tough decisions, had knowledge of our community's history, and knew where we were heading. Adding all this together, one quickly realizes why Fargo came out on top of the flood rather than underneath the floodwaters.

Prior to the catastrophic flood in 1997, Bruce had done his homework, had reviewed where the most likely troubles would come, Bruce then worked with the other city managers. Because of this great team, our city was spared a disaster like occurred in Grand Forks, North Dakota, a city only 60 miles to our north.

As Mayor of Fargo, Bruce has to make many tough decisions. Not once, to my knowledge, has he made a decision which benefited one of his friends above our community.

Bruce treats people fairly, logically, and equitably. As a consequence his friends stand by him.

One can develop great personal relationships from community involvement. Now is the time for you to take action! You will find community activities can help your faith grow along with your friendships.

Chapter 10

FAITH/HOPE

"If ye have faith as a grain of mustard seed, ye shall say unto this mountain, remove hence to yonder place; and it shall remove; and nothing shall be impossible unto you."
From the Bible; book of Matthew, Chapter 17 verse 20

Whether we want to accept it or not, we all live our life based on some level of faith. We flip a switch having faith that the lights will come on. Believing we will not be electrocuted in the process. We eat our vegetables having no idea what happens to them once they are in our stomach, but we have faith they will be good for us. Stop to ponder all the wonderful aspects of your life which are built upon the simple belief things will work out as you plan. Consider the many aspects of our daily lives we believe will continue uninterrupted. Mankind has not always been able to expect life will go on uninterrupted day after day. At one time in our history we didn't understand where a volcano came from. All of a sudden, out of the blue, something would happen. Hot lava would spew out of a mountain and our world would seem to come to an end.

You catch a terrible cold, yet you have the belief your body will overcome this intruder. A belief based solely on an unseen faith. Loose your faith that the cold will end and eventually a cold will kill you.

Faith/Hope

Numerous studies have been done concerning people's faith in everlasting life as expounded in the Bible. Study after study has shown people with a strong belief in a higher being are able to overcome illnesses faster. People who believe in an after life find greater joy in their lives here on earth.

How strong your faith is depends upon your experiences and how deep your desire to lead a fulfilling life.

On March 20, 1998, when I suffered my stroke, Cynthia found me lying on the floor. She called for paramedics, and then sat down to pray. Throughout my seven-week hospitalization she maintained her sanity because of her faith in God. In all the many issues we have faced in life, her faith has remained. Had she found me, sat down in prayer without taking action to call for medical help, my life would have ended right then and there.

Undoubtedly her faith carried her through this trying challenge. Prayer without positive action would only have ended in disaster.

Faith is not a fix-all, but it certainly helps. During any challenge having God on your side is a lot better than not having God with you.

My faith was challenged to its core during the aftermath of my stroke in 1998. Constantly challenging myself in a spiritual sense while observing parts of my life unraveling was difficult.

Faith/Hope

Throughout my illness, Cynthia was guided by her faith. She used God to lean upon. During the many frustrating hours watching a person close to her in pain. During the countless discouragements and arguments that resulted from the illness, she found comfort, guidance and strength through her boundless faith in God.

Perhaps you will never be tested to the limits we were, but by seeking to better understand your personal beliefs you will become a much stronger person. Strength can flow to you through faith.

To have real faith in life you must be willing to take action. You need to flip the switch to turn on the electricity to generate light. Take some action to turn yourself on!

For you to walk in faith you must take action based on what is right. Simply hoping or praying the lights will come on by themselves doesn't make anything happen. Most of all, faith has some basis in your beliefs about God and religion.

The Bible is very clear on the fact that each of us are judged by what we do, not how we believe. If you truly have a deep religious faith, your actions will confirm this faith.

Chapter 11

RELIGION

'But they that wait upon the Lord shall renew their strength; they shall mount up with wings as eagles; they shall run, and not be weary; they shall walk, and not faint."
From the Bible; book of Isaiah, Chapter 40 verse 31

Perhaps you have strong religious convictions. In today's world, not unlike the days of yesteryear, religion is a very delicate subject. We feel the need to demonstrate our belief in God, yet similar to the apostle Peter, we fear the societal repercussions should we acknowledge our belief in God, so instead of following our heart, we deny our faith. Just like Peter did some 2000 years ago.

Too much preaching rarely works. You must strive to create deep religious beliefs within yourself, but you must also recognize that a balance between acknowledging God, and professing your beliefs, must be found for you to be accepted as true and honest.

Throughout my writings and life, my objective has been to achieve this delicate balance between strong belief, openly acknowledging God, but not preaching. Sprinkled delicately in my writings are stories and quotes from the Bible. A person who doesn't recognize my convictions to God hasn't really read what I've written or listened to me speak.

Religion

For my life, this balance has worked well, rarely is someone offended by my religion. Perhaps there is not enough strength in my convictions for your taste. Only you can judge for yourself.

You need to discover what religious convictions are correct for your life. Should you wish to be ordained as a minister it is not too late to take action to follow your desires.

Religion, like any other aspect of our life, will help define the people you associate with and the relationships you develop during your life.

Does your God suggest to you that you need not follow his teachings? Perhaps you don't think you need to do anything but believe. The Ten Commandments are items which we must or must not do. Religion affects almost every area of our lives; most especially your religious beliefs affect your relationships with others.

Positive examples of the spiritually strong abound in our society. On North Broadway in Fargo stands Plymouth Congregational Church, a quaint inner city church, with stunning internal warmth. The Reverend James (Jim) Martin is pastor of this church. Jim is a perfect match for this congregation. He is warm, considerate, articulate and a very caring man. Certainly some church members want a "Fire and Brimstone" preacher at the pulpit. Each week, Jim attends to the churches needs. He also can be found most days visiting patients in our local hospitals.

Religion

When I was hospitalized for the seven weeks at Merit Care in 1998, Jim visited me frequently. He was always a welcome addition to my day. The care and concern for my well being was seen through Jim's actions, and radiated through his eyes.

You may wish to argue these visits were part of a minister's duty, certainly they are, but the quality, frequency, and commitment of the visits indicate the real belief the person holds in his heart.

Pastor Martin's weekly sermons are designed to promote deeper faith (of course they must). Without fail, a good listener will gain some valuable insight to life from Jim's weekly messages; in addition, his messages inspire people to take action. A clear, honest heartfelt message that creates positive action is far better than a loud screaming voice that does nothing but shake the rafters.

To carry deep religious beliefs, one does not need to jump up, scream, or threaten purgatory. Sometimes the quiet confidence of a deep faith can communicate your beliefs much better than a microphone with loud speakers attached.

Benjamin, Caleb and Berea are taught from the bible daily. When we have tried forcing our children to learn the stories of the Bible, this has created many arguments. Children should learn from the Bible, but forced learning will not work. Quietly following faith can be very effective, forcefully it looses impact.

Religion

Be careful how you set your sails in regard to your religious beliefs, your choices and actions will affect your relationships with almost every person in your life.

It has been said we all hope there is a heaven, but none of us want to die.

Holding on to your religious convictions during times of trouble can be difficult. Perhaps you have been challenged during your lifetime, and have not felt comfort in your personal beliefs. Anyone in any circumstance can grow their personal convictions through observing others, reading the Bible or going to church. Your level of commitment to your religious beliefs is critically important to successfully maintaining a constant level of motivation. As your beliefs grow, you will be able to enhance your personal character, and others will begin to take notice of you. Use your religion as a launching pad for a balanced fulfilling life.

Chapter 12

CHARACTER

'It is better to have character than to be known as a character.'

"Character is the ability to carry forward with a resolution long after the mood in which the resolution was made has left you." Good character means continuous commitment. Always doing what you say you're going to do, always following through with your plans and statements.

You want to develop into a person known to always do what you say.

Many of our great national leaders of the past, possessed the ability to always complete a commitment. Abraham Lincoln, George Washington, Benjamin Franklin to name just a few are certainly men of great character. Possessing the level of personal integrity, each of these great individuals had, takes a huge commitment to life. No matter what your character is today, you can develop honorable personal character by always doing the right thing when confronted with a challenge.

On September 11, 2001 the United States was attacked by terrorists. President George W. Bush was faced with a huge tragedy. Fortunately for our country, our President rose to the occasion and worked to unite our country. President Bush demonstrated great personal character and a

Character

commitment which gave credit to the office of President.

Keep in mind, Lincoln fired more than one of his generals. Washington took great risk against England. Franklin built industries and inventions through risk.

Always facing tough decisions, in the long run, the character of these three men remains intact. Why was Franklin going out in a rainstorm with a kite anyway?

By starting a fire department did Franklin plan to start fires?

Did Washington think his men would drown, or did he believe in his cause enough to take this big risk when they crossed the Delaware?

You can see, true character takes commitment to do what is right, and in all likelihood you will be challenged at the time of your decision. Make the long-term choice of good character and you will be motivated to achieve more in life.

If your life is full of going to do's, you probably need a character check. How often you answer a question with I'm going to do....is a good measure of your commitment to character.

Some of your acquaintances in life probably are frustrating to be with as they offer well-intended suggestions of what you are going to, maybe, do together. The quickest way to blast away a child's

Character

enthusiasm is to tell the child we will do it later, or we are going to do it someday…

If you want to be known for your superior personal character, don't make well-intended suggestions. Become a person of commitment in everything. Commitment is just another word for positive character.

Chapter 13

THANKFULNESS

'We all long for the sincerity of praise, for the sincerity of a Thank-You for a job well done.'

The stronger your appreciation for your current life, combined with a strong optimism for a good future helps a person maintain daily motivation. Developing optimism involves some level of thankfulness for the life you have or the life you anticipate having.

When your lawn is full of weeds, the grass does look greener on the other side of the fence. But are you looking at your whole lawn or are you focused on just the weeds? No matter what your station in life you can find things to be thankful about.

Your lawn has weeds, maybe the weeds bother you. Is it not a better approach to be thankful for your lawn recognizing many people have no lawn! Start pulling weeds, start nurturing good green grass. Nurture your heart with personal thankfulness.

A good way to develop thankfulness is to thank those around you for the things they do. Thank your spouse for keeping the car full of gas, especially if you expect your spouse to keep the gas tank full. Showing appreciation to others can help you develop thankfulness within yourself.

Thankfulness

It is possible by showing appreciation to those around you to become frustrated. Perhaps you thank your spouse for washing the clothes, for earning a paycheck, for loving the kids, for helping at school. How do you respond if your spouse rarely reciprocates with thanking you for what you do? I have seen this happen many times, the lack of mutual appreciation in a marriage is disastrous. Sooner or later one partner in the marriage feels unappreciated. This is just one of the many reasons for our high divorce rate today.

If thankfulness in your marriage is one-way, obviously your spouse has a problem. Don't give up, give in! Start thanking yourself and God for the good things you do. You can develop a "self thankfulness' by looking within, by becoming aware of the good things you have, the good things you do, you will become more thankful for your life and this thankfulness will lead you to a more motivated day.

Receiving thanks is as important as giving thanks. One way to help your personal relationships is through sincere honest compliments. Sincerity is absolutely necessary, empty praise will be identified as hollow.

When suggesting this philosophy of showing thanks to a woman, I once received the reply; "You don't want me to lie about my feelings do you, what if it just doesn't matter that much to me?" This response was very troubling. She obviously is very self-centered. Is it really lying to thank someone for doing something good?

Thankfulness

Lying is bad, but any appreciation expressed to others is a positive step toward enhancing a relationship.

A stronger word for thankfulness is gratitude. Developing a true sense of gratitude for yourself and those around you will lead you to a much happier existence. Roll the word gratitude around in your mind. Does this give you a good feeling inside? Having a sense of gratitude for our lives helps each day become more and more exciting.

By building a level of thankfulness for your life, you can begin a journey towards greater personal ethics and higher standards of integrity. Sometimes, no matter how thankful you may be, you come to a crossroad in your life and find yourself in a challenging situation. Answers to life's difficult questions are not always easy to find on our own. If you are struggling to make the right decision on an issue, don't be afraid to seek help.

Chapter 14

HELP

'Insanity is doing the same things over and over expecting different results!

We all face circumstances in our lives where we need to seek professional help. If the tire on your car goes flat, you need to see a repairman. Maybe you can find a way to create a temporary fix yourself, but in all likelihood, if you want the repair to last, you need to employ a professional mechanic.

We, especially those of us in the upper Midwest, have developed an attitude which creates the belief we should be able to work through our problems ourselves. This tough-guy individualism can, and does lead to unnecessary frustrations in life. Many people are employed in our society today, just to help people with their personal issues.

Most people you consider your friends will probably be more than glad to lend you a helping hand in times of need, but when real trouble looms, find the best professional you can. During the council of many individuals over the years, my approach often has been to refer people to those more capable than me. My expertise lies in goal setting, business planning, business finance, and personal finance. In these areas, I can help people. Handling some issues is a chore for me, and my qualifications are not that of a psychologist, so reliance on assistance professionals allows me to feel best when

Help

suggesting to those searching for help that they find a professional. Ask me what to do about a broken air conditioner, and the only answer would be to recommend a refrigeration repair business.

Real Estate transactions are a very common occurrence for both businesses and in personal life. Dacotah Paper has bought and sold a number of properties over the years. We feel we are very good at managing as well as upgrading industrial warehouse space. There is a certain level of pride at being able to negotiate and close a real estate transaction independently. Recently we were involved with purchasing a building in our area. The purchase agreement was essentially done, price determined, and transaction nearing completion. Everything appeared to be in perfect order, so we anticipated a smooth, quick transaction. Jon Strinden, a very astute local lawyer and close personal friend of mine was called to take a look at the documents. Jon agreed everything appeared to be in order, but he suggested we look at one particular sentence which if left as written might not give us complete liability protection. As we neared the final days of the transaction, Jon caught one word on the deed which made him uncomfortable. This one word could make a big difference to us if we were to uncover an unrecorded mortgage on the property at a later date. We made the changes Jon suggested. Ask for help or seek out the best professional to assist you in times when you are tempted to go it alone, and most especially during times when you are not completely knowledgeable on how to handle a situation in

Help

your life. Perhaps everything on our real estate transaction would have worked out fine without professional help. Knowing you've done the absolute best job and have received the most knowledgeable advise will keep you motivated to tackle important jobs during your lifetime.

During the composition of this work, our economy was soft, resulting in me spending ten, twelve, fourteen-hour workdays concerning my duties at Dacotah Paper in addition to writing. My determination to complete this book along with my extra efforts at Dacotah Paper Company put a strain on the relationship between Cynthia and myself.

At one point, communication between us was not appropriate. We disagreed too much about too many things, and the children became affected.

Put your head down, throw yourself into the problem and figure out a way to overcome the trouble was my natural response to the situation. One Saturday morning it dawned on me my natural response mechanism wasn't working towards conflict resolution.

It was time for me to seek advise from friends. I sent an intimate message to a group of my friends. Not surprisingly, many suggested we seek counseling.

An appointment was made with a marriage counselor. By choosing to utilize the professional advice we received, our marriage can be moved

Help

towards happiness. Without professional help what other than arguments could we expect from ourselves?

During our work together to better our lives in conjunction with the counseling we received, we created a number of positive experiences for ourselves. The children started to become more happy and responsive.

Trying to resolve the issues between us by taking the same approach would probably have ended in disaster. Why any of us think we can find conflict resolution by approaching the conflict in the same manner in which it started is crazy. In times of trouble, seek out those who can help you. Rarely will a problem be solved without some new approach. Old ways rarely fix old problems.

Once again, it is the choice to take action positive or negative which determines the eventual result.

Chapter 15

TEMPTATIONS

'One can always rationalize the decision to stray from the path of righteousness.

Where you are in your life today, only you can assess. Perhaps you are approaching a fork in the road of life. Perhaps the seasons for you are changing.

During times of stress and change, it is critical to assess your life's ambitions to help determine if making a change is the result of your choice for a better life or the result of pure temptation. At times, we are all tempted in our lives. The young child who walks through the candy aisle in the store is temped to sample a piece or two. Some succumb to the temptation and steal the candy. Others, for reasons we typically attribute to parental guidance, choose not to steal the candy.

As we age, temptations grow and our propensity to fall victim to temptation becomes more and more a matter of our commitment to our lives. If we have a plan for our lives complete with goals, we are much more likely to make good, moral choices.

As we age, how do we choose to deal with our expense accounts at work? Is it easy to forget a few items on our tax return? If you have made a commitment to your life, choices during tempting times will be much easier.

Temptations

If a contemplated change in your life feels right and enhances the picture you hold of your future, the change is probably good, even though you may wonder if you are being tempted. For every contemplated change in your life, you should ask yourself if the item in question is easy to decide and if your choice will move you towards the life you desire. If you struggle with the question, your conscience is telling you something about it doesn't fit right. A mental struggle clearly should suggest to you to try a different approach. Having a picture of your future will also make it easier to determine if the change enhances that picture. Certainly as you develop this picture of yourself you will want it to show your life as ethical and filled with personal integrity.

Some people mistakenly believe that poverty creates crime and leads to decisions to succumb to temptations of theft, violence, dishonesty, etc. Falling victim to temptations in life are not dictated by wealth or social status. Your beliefs, along with your values, determine how easily you will fall victim to bad temptations in life.

Chapter 16

ETHICS AND INTEGRITY

'Doing things right is far easier than doing the right things.'

Each of us has a different opinion of what the right response to a given situation should be. Developing a strong sense of ethics takes conscious effort. One must internalize the desire to respond to every challenge in life with flawless integrity. Ethics are developed consciously. Unethical responses often occur without thought of their consequences.

Of paramount importance is to determine what level of personal integrity and honesty you want to maintain.

It is easy to use social norms or racial bias as an excuse for unethical behavior. Perhaps you discover your old automobile has defective seat belts. Do you call the person who now owns the car, or do you hope nothing happens, and if something does happen, pray you don't get called upon for answers? After all, the car manufacturer is really at fault. A situation similar to this occurs every day. One cannot easily answer what the real ethical response would be. Almost any action can justifiably be explained away.

Ethics are probably the most fascinating aspect to develop in your pursuit of constant motivation. If you are relatively confident you will respond to bad situations in a purely ethical manner, you will

Ethics and Integrity

be more likely to look forward to each event in your life, even if you know a conflict of opinion is certain to arise.

Unethical behavior is easy to explain away. Perhaps you are unmarried, in a non-committed, but seemingly permanent relationship, do you seek out other members of the opposite sex to spend time with? After all, you're not committed. A basis for differentiating between pure ethical behavior or unethical behavior is at hand. How you were raised as a child can greatly influence you in the circumstance.

If you have developed a sense of ethics you will either not pursue additional company or let your non-committed friend know the relationship between the two of you is at the end of its road.

Should you break the trust of this non-committed relationship, you will live forever haunted by your lost personal integrity.

When I first met Cynthia, I was involved in a tremendous relationship with another woman. Recognizing a challenge to my integrity was at hand; my mother and I went for a long walk. My mother has the highest standards of integrity. During the walk, my mother stated to me, "You must choose which woman you want to pursue."

No gray area. I needed to simply choose. Taking this advice to heart, the old relationship was ended by me before my relationship with Cynthia

Ethics and Integrity

progressed. Fortunately my mother offered the right help.

The freedom of knowing a new relationship with Cynthia could be pursued honestly with complete personal integrity allowed our relationship to move towards our eventual marriage.

Had I chosen to try to play both sides of the fence everyone would have suffered. The old relationship would have been clouded by deceit and mistrust. A new relationship would not have been allowed to blossom and grow with my personal integrity at risk.

Imagine the different result had my mother said, give it some time, test both sides of the water, and don't jump in without first checking with your toes. My mother has integrity so she gave me clear direction. Her help has allowed my integrity to remain intact for a lifetime.

The strength of your ethics are largely determined by how solid your personal values are. Do you have a clear picture of the difference between right and wrong? If you can take home some office supplies from work when convenient for you, do you really think you can expect your children to not steal? Is it acceptable for Mr. Ignorant to smoke, drink, or swear a blue streak, but yet a punishable offense for your children to swear, smoke or drink? Tell your children, "its only just Mr. Ignorant, so it's fine for him under his life's circumstances", and you have effectively demonstrated to your children they can swear,

Ethics and Integrity

smoke or dink too. Rest assured your children will test the waters or challenge you when they perceive weak values.

Personal values which are not concrete are quick sand. Having quick sand values will eventually pull you down, maybe even cause you to drown.

Looking towards the future, Benjamin, Caleb and Berea will be taught a depth of integrity, ethics and honesty which will be uncompromising. How do you want to live and what do you plan to teach your children?

Personal integrity boils down to how you deal with yourself inside, which determines how you respond to ethical challenges in your life.

Generally you will admire a person's integrity because they posses a trait that you feel you have the potential to exhibit yourself. You are drawn to and admire people who demonstrate the level of integrity in a matter which you, yourself believe you are possible of demonstrating.

You can gain every possible trait for the highest level of personal integrity. All it takes is commitment to do the right things combined with a conscious effort to have high standards. However, to have the integrity you desire, you must move from potential to possession through your actions.

Caleb, our son, has a love of life and exhibits a true lust for living. He seeks excitement, laughter

Ethics and Integrity

and these traits show through continuously in his actions. This is easy for me to see as a completely congruent life. Caleb demonstrates these traits by letting them show through his actions. In a good way, he wears his emotions on his shirtsleeves. Some people may feel he is not responsible or too happy go lucky. Some may feel he needs to be better controlled. Give the little guy his big wheel in the dead of winter and he will be crashing through snow banks or riding the top of his snow mountain with great enthusiasm. My admiration and understanding of Caleb is based on recognizing his level of personal congruency. Consequently, we have developed an outstanding relationship. In the most difficult situations we have always been able to communicate with each other. Our relationship is built upon trust and integrity. We understand each other, and seek to support our lives. We are always honest with each other.

An honest response to every question requires a great sense of personal ethics. Suppose you are a mechanic working at the local garage. The owner suggests you add a charge to a repair bill for repairs that were not done. Can you actually refuse to do this and maintain your employment? What if you say you will add the charge, lie to the garage owner, but fail to add the subject cost to the bill? Maybe you break the billing machine? Are you acting in an ethical manner with anything you choose? If you do add the charge or promise to add the charge, and fail to add it, you have chosen to sacrifice your integrity. The only way to

Ethics and Integrity

maintain your integrity is to find a new job. If you do not find a different job soon, you know you will eventually have to find another job because this garage is destined to fail as a result of the owner's dishonesty.

A business associate of mine questioned me about how to handle a dishonest expense reimbursement request. He wondered if he should fire this person. Absolutely, was the reply he received. He was in a no win situation; either fire a good producer which could result in lost revenue, or live with the constant feeling of mistrust. Unfortunately the business associate's sense of compassion was causing him conflict in his decision. The man was discharged which was the right thing to do for every party involved.

Expense accounts are a difficult issue for most organizations and can be very tempting to the employee. At one time my employer, (not Dacotah Paper Co.) had me checking expense accounts as part of my job duties for a government military program. Most team members needed to secure secret clearance from the FBI, some top-secret clearance. Going through the expense accounts one particular individual showed multiple trips between our plants for many days of the week. I questioned the validity of the expense reimbursement request. The individual went to another team leader complaining about me. The other team leader then gave me a stern lecture which went something to the effect; "This guy has the FBI and CIA going through his closets and you hassle him about a few dollars in mileage?

Ethics and Integrity

Leave him alone!" The lesson was learned well. Today, if any expenses are questioned at my company, we check them out with a fine tooth comb. If we discover any person is cheating, we discharge the perpetrator. Looking back, it does seem ridiculous that I would challenge an expense request from a man handling sensitive government equipment who maintained top-secret clearance with the FBI, but if he would have cheated on his expenses, would he have released sensitive information about our project?

Ethics and honesty are very closely related. Choose your path carefully. Only an ethical and honest approach will keep you motivated.

It is usually not possible to keep excited about your job, your spouse, yourself if you have been a cheat. We have all witnessed the child who cheated on a test in school, then became "uninterested" in the teacher or subject. Trying to hide from the guilt, it is easier to become disinterested. Soon the teacher becomes the culprit in the student's eyes. After all, if the teacher knew his subject, the student would have been interested in learning the material! Unfortunately through the process of disinterest, the student finds himself struggling with a bigger and bigger lie.

Chapter 17

HONESTY

'You never have to remember what you said if you tell the truth.'

Being truthful to yourself is as important, as is being truthful to others. Not everyone tells the truth, some people lie. Some people tell lies a lot of the time. Unfortunately liars are liars and there is little you can do about it, but you don't have to be a liar yourself.

It is amazing how people who frequently lie, have short memories, often forgetting conversations or forgetting commitments. Caught in their lies, the person simply "forgets" the event took place. Liars are liars, and we can't necessarily change them.

Sometimes we all get frustrated by a lie someone has willed upon us. Maybe we say, "Wallace shouldn't have lied." No doubt it would be better had "Wallace" not lied, but you can't change him, if Wallace is going to lie, he is going to lie. What about you?

Of course, carrying honesty to the extreme, in our society, is not a good approach. You notice a co-worker in the most ugly shirt you could imagine. Appropriate behavior does not call you to tell your co-worker your feelings. Should your co-worker ask you if you like the shirt, be careful what you respond, if you lie by telling them you love it, you may find a duplicate for you in your next birthday

Honesty

present! Tactfulness in these situations is very important. Perhaps the shirt looks good on them or the material looks comfortable. A host of honest approaches exist. Tactfully you can be truthful.

How big was that fish you caught?

Certainly we all embellish events to an extent, but passing the line of embellishment to outright lying is not necessary. There is a big difference between sharing a story versus giving a real example!

You can be honest in every situation. You don't need to be brutal to your friends, you can embellish when storytelling without being dishonest. Make sure you clarify that you are telling a story, not giving a real example.

If you are honest with yourself and others, you will be much more motivated to work with people.

Being honest with yourself involves accurately assessing your activities as good or bad. Accurately assessing your responses to daily events as correct or incorrect. If you are five foot two inches tall weighing two hundred sixty pounds, telling yourself you weigh one-twenty is not smart or honest. If you weigh two sixty you will not be motivated to look in a mirror simply by telling yourself you only weigh one-twenty! Your brain knows you are lying!

Honesty

The right self-talk is to say, "I <u>will</u> weigh one-twenty by (Your date of choice) then take action to move your weight down. By choosing the right approach in your self-talk, you will be motivated to take the actions necessary to achieve your desired weight. You will be motivated to look in the mirror as you progress towards your desired weight goal.

Negative self-talk or negative self-honesty can be very destructive to your attitude. Maybe you are a liar. When you lay your head down at night, don't say to yourself, "I am a liar." Similarly, don't say to yourself "I am always honest." Either type of self-talk is destructive. You most certainly can remember at least one time when you were honest. Take the opportunity to set your standards to become honest. Remind yourself of the time you were honest, commit to setting an objective to dealing with a specific issue honestly again. Recognize who you are, determine who you want to be, be proactive, make changes and take action and you will be motivated to become who you want to become.

Over time you can teach yourself to be honest and do the right things in life. One way to strengthen your own self-image, and positively enhance your self-talk is through teaching others.

Chapter 18

TEACHING

"Once you become knowledgeable enough to show others how to use their talents for success, then you may be called master."

To be a teacher to others in this world is a noble ideal. Without teachers and coaches we would not benefit from the great society we have today. Whether or not our public school leaders are adequately rewarded financially for their efforts is a topic for debate. Many teachers do an outstanding job. It is likely the current generation of community leaders will develop a better reward system for our outstanding teachers in the near future.

Nearly everyone can relate a positive experience of growth that resulted from time spent with a teacher. We all have the capacity to share our knowledge with others, helping them learn from our experience.

In <u>Personal Riches and Entrepreneurship</u>, the positive effects of Tom and Joan Humphrey were detailed. Tom and Joan found great satisfaction from years of teaching in the Fargo Public School system. Perhaps they sacrificed greater financial rewards, but the internal rewards they each received by sharing their knowledge by teaching far surpassed the economic opportunity loss they felt by not pursuing different careers. Each of them came to school each day excited to help young adults grow. Most of their students

Teaching

benefited far beyond the scope of the classroom materials. These two outstanding individuals demonstrated enthusiasm, concern and constant motivation. Through example, students saw a level of enjoyment in life, which was maintained far outside the boundaries of the classroom.

Perhaps you are not certified to teach in a classroom setting. Regardless of your career choice you can and should seek to teach others. If you are a parent, you have a responsibility to teach your children the beliefs you hold in your heart. You can choose to teach your children through intimidation or inspiring example.

Perhaps you are not a parent, you can teach your co-workers, you can volunteer your time at a local community shelter to teach people in need.

One of the greatest coaches I have ever seen in action is Jim Alexy, my friend and president of Network Associates in Mount Prospect, Illinois. Jim has a natural talent to teach and motivate others to learn. A great deal of my passion for golf comes from the times I spent with Jim on the links. One particular round I struggled with multiple sand shots. Jim suggested we spend 30 minutes practicing together. After 10 minutes of his instruction, 10 minutes of my practice, followed by 10 minutes of Jim praising my correct practice shots, I started to love hitting from the sand. As my game of golf has progressed, sand shots are often my best plays. Of course, Jim's great coaching spans far beyond the game of golf, it is evident in his successful leadership of

Teaching

Network and shows through in his excellent relationship with his wife and their children.

I consider Jim one of my best friends, and a personal confidant of mine. I know that for any crisis in my life, Jim will stick by me and give me any help he can. A true friend, a great coach, and a man of impeccable personal integrity. To be able to consider Jim my friend gives me great feelings of personal well being, or riches. When Jim does a superior job of teaching someone, it is evident in his personal demeanor. He and his student show excitement and enthusiasm.

Many of the most talented employees of Network have blossomed under Jim's tutelage. One particular man often stumbled through presentations to the shareholders of Network. Shortly after Jim arrived at Network, the man's presentation skills dramatically improved. I complimented the man. He smiled broadly at my compliments, but quickly added, "Yes, but Jim makes us practice together the night before the meetings now." With some simple pre-meeting coaching Jim had helped this man shine. The man probably didn't like having to practice, but he moved from stumbling to shining which must have been mighty motivating!

When I was facing marital issues, Jim looked me straight in the eye and said "Matthew, you two have been through a lot, get some marriage counseling together." Advice like this from a trusted friend like Jim made taking the counseling step much, much easier.

Teaching

In the fall of 2001, Cynthia was asked to teach Sunday School at our church. She asked me to participate. She loves to share God's word, my love is to teach. It was not an exciting proposition to me, but as in past experiences it was necessary to respect her commitments. We started teaching, she taught most of the time. Soon my attitude changed and each of the kids in our class became fun to observe. My motivation to participate sky rocketed as we learned together. It is usually very easy to become involved at a modest level of teaching others. Give teaching a try, you will enjoy it, you will develop a deeper appreciation of people who choose to teach as their profession.

Teaching others brings great satisfaction and will help you maintain your motivation to get going each morning. Being a good teacher will almost always enhance personal relationships.

AN EAGLES RESPECT

The Eagle is a great bird, why we respect an eagle is perhaps an interesting challenge. Why we respect our teachers is more obvious. The following parable helps me better respect both teachers and Eagles. Consider the story and how you may grow to become like the Eagle yourself.

One day a group of birds gathered to decide which bird was the best.

First the chicken clucked around in a circle and claimed to be the best because of her eggs.

Next a turkey charged through the group to demonstrate how strong and powerful he was.

Then a blue bird flew high in the sky to demonstrate her great ability and beauty.

A goose rose above the blue bird honking loudly to prove his superiority.

Finally, the group of birds all looked up to see an eagle gracefully flying higher than the rest had flown. Surely this quiet powerful bird must be the most respected for his great ability to soar to the heavens the birds thought.

But wait, asked the barn swallow, what is that little thing up by the eagle right now?

The barn swallow had pointed out a little sparrow which the eagle had carried up to the heavens on his wing. The little sparrow then flew down and joined the group of birds in personal delight of his first flight.

The birds decided the eagle was the most grand bird of all, but was it because of his ability to fly, or was it because of his willingness to teach others to fly?

Chapter 19

PERSONAL RELATIONSHIPS

'For better and for worse, in sickness and in health.'

The human being is largely a social animal. We choose to associate with others like us, we marry, procreate our species, yet we have amongst us those who choose to kill. Personal Relationships can create great joy, but they can create great sorrow.

How we go about choosing our mate (spouse) is a fascinating study in our behavior. What attracts us to that supposedly right one person? What allows some couples to sustain their marriage while other marriages end in disaster after only a month or two? When marrying, does the couple take their vows seriously or are they merely an old fashioned ideal?

Any type of relationship takes great efforts to sustain. Most of us approach life from different perspectives.

Benjamin, our oldest son and I have a magical relationship. Regardless of the issue or event, we both know deeply the other's needs and desires are put first in the relationship. As early as six years old, Benjamin would ask to help me sort out my daily problems. He deeply wanted to learn about the events of his dad's day. Benjamin approaches life in a logical, compassionate,

Personal Relationships

caring manner, and he can be relied upon to help in almost any situation.

Fortunately for both of us, we both believe our love and bond to one another is unbreakable.

Caleb, our second son, is very emotionally charged. He looks at all of life as fun. He is a constant builder and has unquenchable curiosity. Caleb comes to his Dad to resolve the many issues in his emotionally charged life, because he recognizes Dad will approach the issue as unbiased a way as possible. He is fascinating to observe as he transforms from an emotionally charged youngster to a logical, philosophical, reflective individual. The fun Caleb adds to almost every event inspires all of us.

Berea, our third child, and only daughter, is a curious and energetic little creature. She demands Cynthia's time and complete attention. Berea's actions show she knows she always comes first with her mom. It is pure fun for our whole family watching this little one blossom.

On our walls at home hang picture collages of a few of our family vacations. We have had a tremendous amount of fun seeing our country and being together. A family event like a vacation does not happen without commitment and effort to work together.

Simply by watching others as they interact you can form ideas of how your interpersonal

Personal Relationships

relationships can be enhanced to better match what you want for your life.

During a lifetime we all enjoy some great friendships and probably have had disastrous relationships.

We spend a lot of time at the Fargo Country Club. One can frequently find Benjamin, Caleb and I at the pool, on the driving range, playing a round of golf, or just generally enjoying the club. Considered the most prominent of golf clubs in the city, membership is comprised of many long time Fargo residents, along with a variety of other members.

It is fascinating to watch the older couples at the club, many who demonstrate their lifelong love for one another with their on-going attention to one another as well as their appropriate demonstrations of affection. The club, without a doubt is typical of many similar well-established country clubs across the nation. What is really thrilling to observe is the still married, still in love, devoted to family, couples which exist.

Some families at the club remain together during events while others seek social separation from their spouses and children. The families with the best relationships remain together. If you are holding the hand of your spouse and children, do you need to be concerned about who they are with?

Personal Relationships

A true friend is there when you are on the top, is there with you when you fall, and is with you on your way down in life. Put another way, a friend is the one coming in to see you when everyone else is leaving.

David Silbergleit is my great friend. He always has time to share. He always offers encouraging words of advice. When I was hospitalized in 1998, David visited each Sunday morning so my family could attend church. Seeing his friend in terrible medical condition was no treat for him, yet he was there week after week.

On one particular Sunday, we became involved with an exchange about retirement planning with one of the medical staff. At one point, David exclaimed; "Matthew, you are a genius, that is absolutely right!" Keep in mind, for weeks I had heard I couldn't think straight and many of my thoughts were unreliable. David's suggestion of genius was honest, sincere, and very important for me to hear at this stage. A better friend would be hard to find in this world.

Each member of our family frequently indicates to each other we are friends. Having your spouse and children as friends is an extra bonus in your life. You should take action to include all of your family in your friendship circle.

Is it not better to consider your spouse as a close friend, and value that relationship in consideration of your love for one another?

Personal Relationships

While growing up in the 1960's, our family included my mother's mother. Her husband had died unexpectedly and Grandmother Ruth Erickson was invited to join our household by my parents.

Reflecting back upon the years, my father had to have exercised tremendous self-discipline and he must have deeply desired to have his marriage survive in order to accept his mother in law into his household. She lived with us from the early 60's until her death in the mid 70's.

Grandmother Ruth Erickson had a tremendous influence on all of our lives. She would play with us, comfort us, and teach us. She was a person who greatly influenced my level of competitiveness. She enjoyed life immensely and liked to win. When we would play a game of cards or a game of checkers, she invariably would win, but in the process she explained the right decisions to make so I would do better the next time. If anyone was ever to win against her it was a true victory. She never let another person win. She was a "grand" grandmother to have. My life has experienced more winning because of her. My desire to win was greatly influenced by her teachings.

My mother recognized her good fortune to be able to offer our home to her mother, and she frequently expressed her appreciation to my father. My fathers actions in regards to Grandma Ruth demonstrated he wanted his marriage to last.

Personal Relationships

Think of the woman whose husband has told her, "I did fine without you before, and I don't care if we get divorced or not." This is a terrible perspective, the woman unfortunately has to face each day wondering if her husband will really fight to keep their marriage alive or will leave at the first sign of trouble. Their marriage vows probably include the words, for better and for worse. Once worse times occur, unfortunately husband or wife will probably decide to leave.

Today, divorce is a common rather than uncommon occurrence. Observing couples together, one can quickly assess the completeness of their marriage. Are they together or simply in the same area, or are they in reality far apart? Do they hold hands? Do they share laughter together? Relationships are hard to maintain let alone grow day after day. Good relationships take hard work. Laziness in relationships causes failure. To add strength to a relationship, simple gestures like holding hands, a hug, a kiss in public, communicate your love to each other as well as communicating your strength to others who observe you. When was the last time you shared true appreciation to your spouse about something? By making a point of adding small gestures, thank-you's and verbal love notes, you can greatly enhance any relationship. Who do you take the time to dress-up for? Do you dress in a starched shirt and suit for success at the office? Become the slob at home? Do you wear a new dress for a friends visit then show your husband your holey underwear at

Personal Relationships

night? These things do matter, most people, your children, your spouse will notice.

Children can add to a marriage, create a family, or they can destroy a loving relationship. How you act, how you treat each other is never lost in a child's eye. Children do have a way of showing us our deepest truths. Always having been a hard driven competitive person, before becoming a parent, my attitude changed to be sure to let my kids be kids.

Out of respect to everyone in my family and those within my circle of friends, I must constantly remember how difficult it is to be in a relationship with a person like me who always expects the best performance from himself and others in everything.

My childhood was much too short. Kids need a time to have fun and grow up. Finding their own tragedy in life, discovering thrills, learning honesty, as well as learning other characteristics are important parts of growing up.

Caleb, our second son is a fun loving excitable young boy. His knick name if Kamikaze. Turn on a sprinkler and he will delight in running through it. During the middle of winter, Caleb will pull out his big wheel just to crash it through snow banks, laughing all the time. Caleb has the kind of enthusiasm we all would like to keep for a lifetime. Keeping the attitude of letting kids be kids has allowed me to grow to appreciate Caleb more each day.

Personal Relationships

Benjamin, our oldest son, is a fine growing young man. He has an undeniable level of honesty, has character as deep as anyone you could meet, yet he loves to play games. He has a level of conscious thought that few young boys exhibit. His decisions reflect sound logic and a depth of caring for others around him. The fear exists in me that he is growing up too fast, just like his Dad grew up too fast. Fortunately, Benjamin like most kids today, loves electronic games and sports. Considering the desire of letting kids be kids, encouraging these playful activities is much easier for me today than it would have been in years past. As fine of a young gentleman as he is, he also needs to be a kid at times.

Games, sports, the influences of our coaches all help teach us the value of winning in life.

Chapter 20

WINNING

'Being a winner beats being a loser, every time.'

Grandma Ruth Erickson demonstrated through her competitive spirit in the games we played that winning is a lot more fun than loosing. To win you must take action. Do you really want to become a good loser? The only good losers are losers.

As a young boy playing on the local hockey team, we won all but one game for three years of play. As we entered Junior High School, some authority decided we were just too much better at hockey than the other kids, so to be fair, our team was split apart. Now it seemed everyone had a chance to win. Unfortunately a very cohesive group of young adults were split apart for being winners. Instead of creating groups of new winners, multiple groups of losers were created. To none of our surprise the new teams didn't get along, coaches were unhappy, kids started smoking, drinking, and a few took drugs.

Certainly those players who started smoking, drinking or taking drugs can not blame these bad activities on the hockey team split-up. But some of us today think if we would have been allowed to stay together and had the support to win, those misguided players would not have chosen the improper roads they did. To this day, the logic of destroying a winning, cohesive, extremely successful, and good bunch of kids, escapes me.

Winning

Why anyone would feel a group was too good to be together is senseless. Had the group been the school orchestra, the school would never have allowed its destruction. No doubt, a fantastic orchestra would have been paraded from school to school to demonstrate these great winners! A hockey team for some reason needed a more "equitable" approach.

If you are familiar with hockey, the names Bobby Hull and Dave Christian may have meaning to you. Early on, our team skated well against Dave Christians team, we even beat the team Bobby Hulls son played on. You probably know both of these men played in the National Hockey League.

Doug Elliot was the leader of our hockey team. Doug was the very best skater the state of North Dakota has ever seen. When we were split up and not allowed to win, Doug (the best player any of us had witnessed) lost a great deal of interest in the team sport of hockey. Why teach such a rising star that winning and friendship doesn't matter? In reality, was he a Hull, Christian or maybe a Wayne Gretzky? There is little question, he was at, or above the level of these super star professionals. Through a bad decision, someone who didn't even know us managed to help ruin many young boys drive and determination to win, and quite possibly sidetracked Doug from a super successful career in professional hockey. Let people win, reward success, but don't patronize failures.

Winning

To most of us from the winning team, it appeared our school didn't care about us or winning. In retrospect, the decision made was a terrible mistake, the consequences of which were minor but could have lead to a major rebellion from all of us.

Winning is good, build yourself into a winner, it may take more work, it may be more stressful, but there is no doubt a winning attitude is the right attitude.

Chapter 21

STRESS

'The only stress free person is the person in a box six feet under with a Lilly in his hand.'

Stress can be good or bad. The thought of living a stress free life is nothing but an illusion. We do have too much stress in our society. There are ways to reduce your stress, but some stress is necessary for a balanced life.

In the early days of humanity, it is suggested our bodies were trained to fight or to run away from danger. As a result, we developed adrenal glands to boost our energy reserve to face the stress of danger. In case a lion attacked us we had to have the strength to run, hide, climb which we didn't normally possess. Today, our bodies react to stress by utilizing these old adrenal glands. Much theory today suggests stress is bad for the body. It is not stress itself, which is bad, but too much stress for your body can become a disaster over time.

You need to control your stress. You need to assess your life experiences to see under what stress conditions you perform best and under what stress conditions you feel the best, before the event, during the event, and afterward.

If you need to set a clock to wake you in the morning or you will miss work, in the long run a daily routine of getting up in time to arrive at work

Stress

is probably less stressful than getting fired from your job.

No one can tell you how to best respond to any situation. No one can dictate to you what level of daily stress is best for your life. You must assess your life by paying attention to times when you feel you are under too much stress, over time you need to take action to increase or decrease your daily stress to match your optimal performance level. Part of the benefits of growing old is learning to adjust our levels of stress by learning how to best respond to events in our lives.

We say a person grows more patient or mellows out with age. This process is a natural by product of learning how to deal with stress. When we are younger, we have not learned how to effectively deal with the everyday twists and turns life throws at us.

Perhaps we experience our first automobile accident. Our minds catastrophize the accident. Our parents will surely take away the car, maybe even toss us out of the house! After great worry we come to realize our life will go on with the accident eventually being forgotten. A few accidents later, we simply get back in the car, and drive to the repair shop for an estimate. With our age and experience, we discover the proper way to deal with this type of situation. At the time of your first auto accident, you should feel stress! As life goes on, you need to assess for yourself what factors in your life warrant the most dramatic responses.

Stress

Imagining various situations in life can help you establish stress thresholds for yourself.

Consider what would happen if tomorrow you lost your job. Do you worry most about your home mortgage? Will your family fall apart? Assess each component of your life under this imaginary scenario. Those things which worry you most are probably those things in which you feel too much stress already. Take action on those stressful items. Get them to a more livable level for you.

Dealing with stress is an individual decision. How you choose to respond to various events in your life will be up to you.

STRESS INDUCERS

Most of us don't need to increase our daily stress levels, but unfortunately we come in contact with things which do increase our stress. Listed below are things you should avoid.

- Pornography
- Watching crime based television
- Observing any type of violence
- Swearing
- Cheating or lying
- Arguing or fighting
- Drinking caffeine based products
- Eating refined sugar foods
- Hearing sirens (Police, Fire, Ambulance)

Stress

STRESS REDUCERS

If you are feeling too pressured during most days you should find ways you can take simple action to reduce your stress. Here are a few time-tested suggestions:

- Take a slow, deep, full breath of air
- Take a leisurely 20-minute walk
- Take a walk through a safe park
- Tend to a garden
- Read a wholesome book of jokes
- Sit quietly and pet a dog or a cat
- Play catch with a child
- Focus your attention by playing a good game like chess or checkers
- Exercise of almost any type
- Count backwards from 10 to 0 slowly
- Take a short 15-minute nap
- Watch "home" movies of your family
- Look at your baby pictures
- Go to Church
- Pray

Stress

How you deal with life's challenges is your decision. You can experience great stress or do your best to respond optimistically to tough times. Your response mechanisms are guided by your experience, knowledge, goals and attitude.

A home mortgage payment is a perfect example of something that will give each of us different levels of stress. Perhaps you feel a very large monthly payment is no big deal, if you loose your job, you loose the house to the bank and move on. Maybe you have saved your entire life to acquire a home with a low mortgage payment. Possibly the low mortgage payment is a stress inducer every month. You couldn't bear to loose your house.

If you are closer to the second mortgage holder example, start a mortgage pre-payment plan. Have a strong relationship with your bank. Solicit your banker's support to help you pay off your mortgage. Once again, you can take action to find a positive direction in your life. As you pay down your mortgage you are guaranteed to be more excited and more motivated to face each new day. Paying off the mortgage creates more daily excitement and requires a commitment by you to fulfill this goal.

Chapter 22

ATTITUDE

'Face the wind with courage and you can get your sails to take you in ay direction you choose.'

Your attitude makes a big difference. In most every situation you choose how you are going to respond. Every day our attitude affects our life for good or bad. Sometimes a person is faced with a situation which can not be controlled, it is not always easy to be positive in tough situations.

Upon waking up in the hospital after my stroke, I said to my family and friends, "I'll come back better than I was before." Trying to paint a positive picture, trying to keep the proverbial stiff upper lip, I was fooling myself about the magnitude of the challenge. Many days were much tougher than expected. My attitude suffered immensely. There were good days, there were horrible days. Having to take a handful of drugs a day was really disturbing. Always having a good attitude is built into my personal pride. I always considered drugs bad. Refusing to use aspirin for a headache probably helped increase my chance of a stroke over time.

Should you face a time of great discouragement, disaster or injury, don't be too tough to take medication which can help. Also, don't be fooled thinking some pills can make your troubles go away or make you the happy go lucky person you think would be good.

Attitude

Medication will not significantly change your attitude about life. Your attitude is your responsibility. If for some reason your body (brain) fails to produce the right chemical balance, talk to a doctor. If your outlook is poor, try looking to the balance challenge found a little later on, you may discover the direction you need to take to improve your attitude.

A life-long hater of drugs, even prescription drugs, I was too proud to think drugs were necessary. When my last medication was dropped, we were all mighty thankful. Our positive attitudes reflect both the thankfulness of having to take no drugs currently along with being thankful for having drugs available when needed.

In retrospect, my initial response was right. Through trial, frustration and lots of help, life has become better for me and my loved ones.

Some of the major keys to building a good attitude are building upon the segments of this book. Most positive motivation results from a combination of a good attitude, desire and positive action.

A good attitude is built by having the ability to look forward to a better future. Strong goals are the best way to develop a positive forward-looking life.

Chapter 23

GOALS; Segment 2

'With goals you choose your destination......Without goals any road will do.'

Having significant goals is critical to personal success.

Goal planning is a relatively simple process. First, one needs to decide on the end result (the goal). Then, when you want that result (the achievement date). After deciding what you want to achieve, you need to set a time line with intervals which provide smaller goals or steps you need to take on your journey to the main goal. Without goals, one simply wanders through life with little purpose to each day.

After you have set a goal with a date for accomplishment, you need to identify what resources you need to acquire to achieve the goal.

Next identify any barriers that exist which you need to overcome to achieve your goal or schedule.

Then determine a plan of action to acquire the resources you need, and a plan of action to use them to achieve your goal. Written goals produce greater results.

The size of your goals are very important. Goals need to be big to have meaning, but they have to be achievable to inspire action. For example, you

Goals; Segment 2

may want to own your home by the time you are forty. If you make that goal today at age twenty-eight, you have set a big, achievable goal.

In the homeowner example, let's assume you are twenty-eight, married with children and have a 30 year home mortgage which requires monthly payments of $900.00 per month. Evaluating your goal you realize you have over eleven years of hard discipline to achieve your goal of no mortgage by age forty. You or your spouse commit to taking care of the children three nights a week. The other commits to an extra part time job three nights per week for four hours per night. Expected earnings are about $6.50 per hour after taxes. Instead of making monthly mortgage payments equaling $900.00, you add your part-time pay on a regular basis paying $1,238.00 per month on your mortgage. Next you check with your banker. You will discover at this higher payment plan, it will still take you over 12 years to pay off your mortgage. Now you need to reassess your goal. What if you work part-time and extra 4.5 hours per day an extra 3 days per week allowing you a monthly payment toward your mortgage of $1,280.25. By doing so, you can own your home mortgage free in twelve years. You can achieve your goal with the right discipline.

Twelve years is a long time, twelve years of working two jobs takes real commitment. If a mortgage free home is important to you. You can achieve it!

What happens if your part-time job comes to an

Goals; Segment 2

end before the twelve years is up? What happens if during the first few years you discover the time away from home at night negatively affects your family too much? Both of these are reasonable questions. Both questions you probably should anticipate. The answer is at the time that these events occur, you need to reassess your goal of a mortgage free home by age forty. You discuss the relative importance of each effected aspect of your life (part time job, family, home mortgage). Then reassess your goals to determine the most important goals under the current environment in which you live.

The story from Chapter 6 about my son Benjamin captures the essence of good goal setting, so it is repeated here.

When my son Benjamin was nine years old he entered the longest drive contest at the Fargo Country Club during the fourth of July celebration. The club professional handed him a kids sized ping driver. Benjamin hit the drive 135 yards, his farthest golf shot ever. He was in first place for longest distance until an older boy ousted him. While closing the event the club pro handed Benjamin the microphone and suggested Benjamin should announce, "That Ping driver sure works good Dad!" Later the club pro privately suggested Benjamin had some real golf talent to me. We were both excited about this opportunity. Benjamin likes to be a winner; his dad wants a lifetime golfing buddy.

Goals; Segment 2

Spotting an opportunity to teach the essence of accomplishment through goal setting, we established Benjamin could earn his own Ping driver by doing a job around the house each day, the job chosen by me, for the next three weeks. Three weeks is a long to wait for a golf club to a nine year old. Twenty-one different jobs is a lot of work to a child who is more accustomed to playing his days away.

We both fulfilled our commitments, Benjamin earned his Ping driver. Excitedly, we anticipate the years unfolding as we golf together.

Goal setting can start at any age, goals are essential to a balanced life. Through a process of committed goal setting you can establish the balance you seek for your life.

To Look

Looking forward, one can find excitement in fulfilling dreams and goals.

Looking backward, one can only remember.

Look back, remember and understand, then turn quickly, look forward to what life's wonders can present to those willing to take a chance at living.

The future is bright for those willing to look beyond yesterday's sunset.

Goals; Segment 2

Goal setting can be exciting, though some people find setting goals a challenging process. Most of the people who find goal setting a chore, simply haven't learned where or how to start.

A good plan to start your goals is by creating a dream list for yourself. What do you want to acquire? Who do you want to become? What do you want to look like?

A good place to begin your dream list is by rolling back your mind to the years you were ten to eighteen years old. What were your dreams back then, and what did you enjoy the most in your life? Did you prefer to be indoors or outside?

Consider each of the aspects of the balance challenge from Chapter 22. Dream of each aspect, visualize who you want to be and what you want your life to reflect for each. Try to look to your future.

As you develop your dream list, be careful to keep your aspirations positive and specific. A good goal for body weight is "to weigh 190 pounds by May 4th". An improper goal would be "to loose weight." You must be meaningful and specific. A general, negative statement is hard to internalize or visualize.

Creating a picture in your mind of your goal is a great way to move you towards its achievement. If you can find an actual picture of your goal, place this real picture somewhere you can look at it frequently. Mentally seeing yourself having

Goals; Segment 2

achieved your desired outcome is essentially what visualization is all about.

Perhaps you want to own a luxury automobile. Get yourself down to a dealership, sit in a showroom model, and request a new brochure to take home with you. Write the sticker price on the brochure. Constantly remember how it felt to you to be holding the wheel of that luxury car. Picture in your mind driving that car into your driveway. Put the brochure where you can see it frequently. Once you are prepared in this way, set a realistic date for when you will write a check for the car of your dreams. Next work out the details on how you are going to earn the money so you can write that check on that day.

You should have short-term goals (less than 1 year), intermediate (2 to 5 years) and long term goals (5 years to a lifetime).

As you start your goal achievement program, it's easiest to start with goals which only require your individual efforts to achieve. Once you get used to making your goals a reality, you can move on to goals which need the efforts of others in your life. By first demonstrating you are capable of successfully accomplishing your goals, you will be able to then garner the support of others around you for new bigger goals.

Goals should be stated in a manner which provides positive direction toward something specific. Negative thoughts or avoidance goals are not as effective as moving towards goals.

Goals; Segment 2

Should you wish a better marriage, a good goal would be, "We will build a fun, positive relationship and for the next 60 days I will compliment my spouse on one thing everyday." This positive, move, towards goal will be effective. An ineffective or avoidance goal would be something to the effect, "We will stop criticizing each other so we don't get divorced." Look carefully at the differences in language and judge for yourself which you think will be more effective.

Perhaps you are employed as a sales person at an automobile dealership and want to be the top seller. A good goal would be, "During July I will sell the most cars I have ever sold in one month, earning me the title of top July sales representative." An avoidance or bad goal would be, "No other rep will sell more cars than me in July."

Choose the positive good producing goals for your life, and you are much more likely to achieve what you desire.

Be sure you prioritize your goals by what is most important to you based on your scores on the balance challenge, which follows.

Chapter 24

BALANCE CHALLENGE

'Walking a tight rope is a challenge, falling from a tight rope is a disaster.'

By this point you probably have decided to take action to find the right balance in your life, so you can achieve the life style you dream about.

On the following page is a chart designed to help you establish where you are in regards to some of the various aspects of life we explored in this book. By using this chart, you can determine where you are in your life based on your standards. You should use it to determine what areas in your life you wish to enhance. You should use it as the starting point to guide you towards effective goal setting for your life.

Life Aspect	Todays Score	Your Current Direction ↓ or ↑	Your Long Term Desired Score	Action you can take to move you closer to your Desired Score
Physical				
Mental				
Financial				
Career				
Community				
Faith/Hope				
Religion				
Stress				
Attitude				
Spiritual				
Thankfulness				
Honesty				
Ethics/Integrity				
Teaching				
Relationships				
- Spouse				
- Children				
- Parents				
- Friends				
Stress				
Daily Motivation Level				
Your Over-all Self Rating				

Balance Challenge

How to use the balance challenge:

You should begin by rating yourself today based on your level of satisfaction in each aspect of your life today. Use a scoring system of 1 to 10 with one being not so good, and 10 being perfect. Or, if you prefer use grade scaling of A, B, C, D, E, and F.

Your current direction score is very important to this exercise. Recently have you been improving in this aspect of your life or is it getting worse?? Judge for yourself. Do you like your direction? What matters is how you feel, not how others think you should be. Most of the time you probably want to be getting better or improving. Sometimes getting worse is the right direction for the time.

Perhaps you have determined you are spending too much time with friends at the expense of your family, so consciously you are de-emphasizing this aspect of your life, so it is going down in direction. Do you really want everything going up at once? Is it reasonable to assume your life could be rebalanced so every aspect was going the same direction at the same time? Over a number of years of work everything can get better for you. Sometimes you need to make trade-offs.

Your long term desired score is critical to establishing your goals and setting your direction in life.

Balance Challenge

All 10's is not reasonable unless you are superman or superwoman. You need to assess where you really want to expend your efforts.

Perhaps you want a perfect career, and a perfect relationship with your spouse. By taking action to achieve these perfect states in your life, you can expect you may fall short somewhere else, perhaps you will loose ground either mentally or physically. Maybe a 5, 6, or 7 on each of mental and physical is your long term desired score. You decide what you want.

The object is to achieve the level of life enjoyment which you desire. By finding and achieving the right score in each area for your life you will find daily direction and maintain your personal motivation towards fulfillment during your entire life.

Perhaps at this point in your reading, or even earlier, you have asked yourself if all this effort is worth it in your life. Certainly a valid question that you should ask of yourself in anything you undertake. From personal experience, I can assure you the effort to maintain motivation, seek out a balance for your life, determining what you want are absolutely the best efforts to make for a fulfilling life.

Balance Challenge

Hopefully the examples of George W. Bush, Doug Elliot, Ruth Erickson, Benjamin Franklin, Rev. James Martin, Judy Siegle, Jon Strinden, Jim Wieland, David Silbergleit, Abraham Lincoln, Jim Alexy, Mayor Bruce Furness, Joan and Tom Humphrey, and George Washington inspire you to take action to move your life forward in a positive manner. You can become whoever you want to become!

Certainly to become successful you need to establish what success means to you. Taking the Balance Challenge will help you determine where you are, where you want to go, and will help create the self discipline you will need for your chosen success.

Chapter 25

SELF-DISCIPLINE

'Facing the winds of change, the man stood tall, took action, and succeeded in building his life.'

Most successful people have a high level of self-discipline. They have the ability to keep working on a project or keep striving to achieve a goal even though it seems impossible.

Do you want to build a stock portfolio? It takes self-discipline. Give up the fast food meal for lunch, brown bag it. Maybe a few co-workers will think that you are odd, but in ten years these same people will wonder why your life is so much easier than theirs. How did you figure out how to save so much money when they are broke? Self-discipline and eliminating some of the low value, quick fixes (instant gratification temptations) will help you succeed.

One of the big ingredients to the feeling of personal well-being is the ability to exercise self-discipline.

How my friend (mentioned earlier) could have the discipline to spend a year studying a dictionary amazes me. The strength of his self-discipline is incredible. With this self-discipline he has demonstrated he can undertake any objective and succeed.

The ball game is on, and it's Monday night. Do you grab a bag of chips and watch the game, or

Self-Discipline

do you sit at your desk to rework your financial projections. Either option will take up about the same amount of time. Obviously, only the second option will bring you closer to the success you desire. Only one of these options takes self-discipline. The more you feel you deserve free time in your own mind, the less likely it is you are exercising the self-discipline to become successful.

Accomplishment, success, and personal riches flow to those who don't quit.

It is hard to separate motivation from self-discipline. Self-discipline is the ability to command yourself from within to take the steps necessary to do things on a daily basis. Self-discipline and motivation are very closely related.

By determining your desires, interests and establishing goals, you create a sense of self-interest. This self-interest helps to urge you on toward your desired outcome each day. Without a set of goals for accomplishment, it is hard to create perpetual motivation. Self-discipline results naturally from this perpetual internal motivation.

Review some of the major accomplishments of your life and you will discover you were motivated by what you would become or receive through this accomplishment. In all likelihood, your desired outcome could only be achieved through a heightened sense of self-discipline during the process of achievement.

Self-Discipline

During the courtship process between a man and a woman, the many aspects of self-discipline are exhibited. We have all watched this courtship process unfold. The first step after one recognizes some initial attraction involves finding a way to meet this guy or girl. Once it is decided a meeting should take place, careful planning usually is employed to ensure we put our best foot forward. When the other person speaks, we actually listen! We pay attention, exercise self-discipline to insure we are not distracted. As the courtship process unfolds, we continue to practice this self-discipline to insure our success, we dream of how perfect the union will be for both of us. We overlook minor obstacles to achieve our courtship goal of a permanent relationship.

Finding the right job involves the same self-discipline as courtship. We decide what we want to do, identify the skills we need, then pursue the skills development within us.

With these two short examples of courtship and a job, you should recognize the fact these processes involve the essence of goal setting. Goals do, in fact, create motivation, direction, and self-discipline which leads you to successfully achieving a good balance for your life.

Chapter 26

DIRECTION

'No matter which road you take, any road will take you to a destination. You must choose the road best suited for you.'

By incorporating the balance challenge into your life, you should find a clearer pathway to making decisions about what you wish to do everyday. Incorporating positive goals for each aspect of life will create positive energy for you, and will provide you with solid direction for your life.

Most of us would prefer to be known as an individual with vision, an individual of strong character as we grow older on this earth. Few of us would be proud to have our grandchildren consider us lost, unproductive and undirected in life.

Success is your choice; you have the tools and ability to seize each day positively! You need to set your course of action to provide the direction in life which will help you create the life you most desire.

Most importantly, recognizing success is your individual choice. How you determine if you are successful must be based on your personal assessment, not someone else's.

Chapter 27

CHOICE

'Either way, by doing something, or by doing nothing, you have made a choice.'

By now you should have recognized a prosperous, fulfilling life is available to everyone who wishes to pursue the life they desire. Good lives don't occur by accident, good lives are created through purposeful action.

You can make the choice to enhance your life by working the balance challenge. Integrating all aspects of a well-balanced life based on your desires will create a great life for you.

You are unique, no one can dictate to you what the most important aspects of your life are to you. Pay attention to what makes you feel like the best person you can be and pursue your own dreams.

One person may place financial success way above personal relationships, health, or anything else. Is this one-dimensional money oriented person wrong in their beliefs? For some people this one dimensional money orientation is wrong. Once again, you decide for your life what is right.

Chapter 28

MORE THOUGHTS

'If you expect more out of life, you'll get it!'

Through reading this book, I hope you have discovered new insights to the importance of life. I hope you have been inspired to achieve a new level of enjoyment through taking action to make your life better for you.

Only by taking action to improve your life can you expect more out of your life. Life can be more exciting and more fulfilling every day.

By knowing yourself, knowing your desires, setting goals and taking action, you can achieve a great life for yourself, uninterrupted by the many bumps you cross over in your life. Build your life by building the life you want. By establishing your own direction, when a freight train threatens you, you will be the one walking away smiling.

If by chance we should meet, I hope you tell me you enjoyed this book, but what I really desire to hear from you is what action you took because of this writing, and the positive outcome in your life which resulted from that action.

More Thoughts

WISHES FOR YOUR LIFE

Strong Faith

Impeccable Integrity

Financial Independence

Enjoying a productive job each day

Abundant Love

Laughter Everyday

Creating Your Own Life's Balance

Chapter 29

DAY BY DAY

'Pray every day like God will take care of you, but work everyday like success is up to you."

Mentally it is easy to think everyday should be a happy one for you and your loved ones. Unfortunately, we live in a world in which we cannot control the outcome of events, nor can we control what others say and do to us.

At a meeting, a particularly motivated, religious and enthusiastic man whom I know and respect looked rather glum to me. After asking him if anything was troubling him, he reassured me his life was fine. Later that night he called saying, "some days you feel great, other days for what ever reason you are just not so enthusiastic. You just need to trust in God and learn to accept how you feel."

Good advice, which we all need to take to heart. Each day we set our course by the actions we take. Our actions demonstrate how much character we have as individuals.

Some days my life looks rather unexciting to me. Is it really necessary to wake before sunrise just to go lift weights to maintain my health? We all face times in our lives where the outlook isn't so good.

We live in a world where we are constantly concerned with others actions against us. Road rage, terrorism, gun-slinging friends. We all need

Day By Day

to learn to better accept the faults of others. We also need to learn to identify the positive aspects of our lives so we don't live in fear.

Maybe you are charged with the responsibility of discharging a fellow employee. Some level of fear is natural in this process. What if the person goes off the deep end, returning with a gun to get you? Most naturally you fear this resulting from your actions to discharge the person, but you must control yourself so you don't go off the deep end in response to these fears.

It is said time heals all wounds, perhaps this is true. Give yourself time to build positive results in each day through your actions. Over time the stress you feel from an unpleasant event will become less. Your choices lead you to a good or bad life day by day. A good life is the result of how well you embrace the positive aspects of life.

Maybe you are saying to yourself something to the effect; sure, it's easy for him to talk about all these good feelings, but my life is different; he's got it made.

Your life is different than anyone else's, but hopefully this book will inspire you to realize from the outside the life of others may look like all roses. The experiences shared from my life are meant to show life can be tough, but as tough as life gets for anyone, a better life is available.

Some days my attitude is bad, when this happens I need to take to heart the lessons shared in this

Day By Day

book. Maybe my head aches, my constant stomach trouble is intensified, or maybe I just have a bad attitude for no good reason. It happens to me and will to you. At these times, we need to be thankful for the good in our lives, have the faith our actions will lead us to a better place, and recommit our thoughts to developing good lives.

Sometimes life is depressing, only through recognizing the good you have can you overcome those negative depressing days. Everyone will face tragedies, to overcome these tragedies you need to prepare a positive outlook for your life. Hopefully the examples contained in this book will inspire you to realize no matter how tough your life seems to be, you can overcome any adversity.

Building constant motivation isn't supposed to be easy, but it is a better choice than unhappiness.

Thankfulness, goals, high ethics, great personal integrity, teaching others all will lead to a better attitude.

As one becomes more successful in life, other people tend to attack this success. Somehow we have created a world where it becomes easy to blame others for our own failures.

My attitude was horrible when I was hospitalized after my stroke. Cynthia was blamed for far too many issues. Day by day, action by action was taken to move our life to a better place.

Day By Day

You will face challenges in your life. For every challenge you face, take some action to counter balance the negative effects. But take positive action! Negative action will usually just result in more harm to yourself and others.

Chapter 30

ACTION IDEA'S

PHYSICAL:

- Stop in at your local hospital to observe patients in the physical rehabilitation gym
- Drive by a nursing home to observe the people in wheel chairs
- Put a few inches of water in your bathtub, dip your toes only in the water, then wiggle your toes, then fill the tub and jump in. Judge for yourself which is more fun, the wiggling or jumping
- Consciously drink a cold glass of water paying attention to how your body feels as you drink

MENTAL:

- Read a few road signs out loud
- Remember one school test you did extremely well on
- Picture yourself in your mind thanking your favorite teacher for your lessons
- Read again your favorite book
- Laugh at a joke
- Go to the library and check out one book and read it

FINANCIAL:

- Visit a luxury automobile dealership just to shop
- Pay off one credit card, keep It paid off

Action Idea's

FINANCIAL (continued):
- Stop at a bank, trade in an old dollar for a new crisp dollar bill, hold the new bill, let how it feels sink in, imagine you had thousands of them
- Read a book on financial planning

CAREER:
- Assess what the best performance you could do at your job
- Assess the company you work for
- Talk to the person you feel is most successful in your job area asking for clues to their success
- Write down ten ways you could help your company grow
- Read a book about your career choice
- Imagine how hard you might work to keep your job if someone else wanted to take it from you. Then go to work

COMMUNITY:
- Volunteer at any community organization
- Call your church, offer 1 hour of your time to help
- Stop at your local Salvation Army, ask where they have the greatest needs, then help them
- Thank your mayor or state representatives just for serving the public

Action Idea's

FAITH/HOPE/RELIGION:
- Read Chapter 10 again
- Pay attention to some little things in life
- Say a prayer-now, any prayer
- Read Psalms Chapter 23 of the Bible
- Go to church this Sunday

HONESTY:
- Tell the truth about one thing today
- Remember the time you told the truth expecting it would hurt

TEACHING:
- Share your knowledge on something with someone
- Find a kid to play ball with
- Talk to a child under 10
- Volunteer to teach Sunday School at your church

RELATIONSHIPS:
- Call a friend just to say hello
- Buy your spouse a single rose and present it personally
- Tell each of your kids you love them today
- Stop by the grave of a loved one, tell them you miss them out loud

Action Idea's

STRESS:
- ➤ Assess what you want to do with your life
- ➤ Laugh hard at a good joke
- ➤ Take a deep breath now and then

THANKFULLNESS/GRATITUDE:
- ➤ Each night say a prayer of thanksgiving
- ➤ Each night, remember at least one good thing that you did that day.
- ➤ Simply say thank you to yourself now and then
- ➤ Smile without warning

Author Biography

Married (Cynthia) and has three children (Benjamin, Caleb, Berea) all residing in Fargo, North Dakota.

Has a Bachelors Degree with Honors, in Economics and Business from North Dakota State University, and a Masters Degree from the Krannert Graduate School of Management, Purdue University.

Named one of five Krannert Scholars by the Krannert School faculty in 1983.

Employed by Texas Instruments, Dallas, Texas and Johnson City, Tennessee during 1983, 1984, and 1985.

Became Operations Manager of Dacotah Paper Company in June of 1985, became Vice President in 1987, Vice Chairman in 1990, President and Chairman of the Board in 1996.

Taught marketing at East Tennessee State University in 1984.

Taught finance, graduate marketing, and entrepreneurship at North Dakota State University during the 1980's, 1990's and 2000.

Served as a Director of the Fargo Chamber of Commerce from 1987 to 1992.

Served as a Director of Network Associates, Inc, Mount Prospect, IL, from 1991 to 1997, completing his tenure as the Corporate Vice Chairman, having also served as Secretary to the Board and Corporate Treasurer.

Served as a Director of Vanity Stores during 1998 and 1999.

Served on the Merit Care Foundation Board of Directors from 1994 to 2000, completing his tenure as Board Chairman in 2000.

Past President, NDSU Commons Club

Authored and published multiple articles on Entrepreneurship.

Published <u>Personal Riches and Entrepreneurship</u> in 2001.

Presently serves as a Director of the North Dakota State University Alumni Association.

Currently a Director for Community First National Bank of Fargo.